The PC Technician's Pocket Field Guide

The PC Technician's Pocket Field Guide

Michael W. Graves

THOMSON

DELMAR LEARNING

Australia • Canada • Mexico • Singapore • Spain • United Kingdom • United States

The PC Technician's Pocket Field Guide

By Michael W. Graves

Vice President, Technology and Trades SBU
Alar Elken

Editorial Director
Sandy Clark

Senior Acquisitions Editor
Stephen Helba

Senior Channel Manager
Dennis Williams

Senior Development Editor
Michelle Ruelos Cannistraci

Marketing Director
Dave Garza

Production Director
Mary Ellen Black

Production Manager
Andrew Crouth

Art/Design Coordinator
Francis Hogan

Senior Editorial Assistant
Dawn Daugherty

NOTICE TO THE READER

Table of Contents

Preface

If you spend your days working with computers in any capacity, then *The PC Technician's Pocket Field Guide* will quickly become your best friend. Within these pages are hundreds of tidbits of information you just won't find under a single cover anywhere else. Installing a hard drive? Check out Part 4, Disk Drives. The jumper settings for the vast majority of IDE and SCSI drives are listed and illustrated. Having problems with your Windows machine booting too slowly? Part 7 lists hundreds of pesky little applications that worm their way into the startup menu, each one adding precious seconds to every boot process you ever endure (and subtracting them from your life). This book shows you which ones you can safely remove. More importantly it identifies potential spyware files and viruses that invade your system.

The topics covered in this field guide include:

- ✔ Setting up shop
- ✔ Basic tools
- ✔ Troubleshooting procedures
- ✔ Installing and troubleshooting hard disks
- ✔ Installing and troubleshooting optical disks
- ✔ Graphics adapters
- ✔ Other hardware issues
- ✔ Operating system issues
- ✔ Network problems

It is not only hardware technicians who will find this book useful. Full of hundreds of charts and illustrations, this book is a must-have for anyone staffing a help desk. Field technicians will find it invaluable, and even network engineers, who inevitably find themselves fighting with the hardware or operating systems from time to time, will reach for it again and again. Use it as a handy reference, but if you are interested in more in-depth information, sidebars will point you to relevant sections of *The Complete Guide to A+ Certification* (ISBN: 1418005665).

Michael W. Graves

Acknowledgements

The common approach to acknowledgements is to pick a family member who hasn't been named, or to butter up your editors by thanking them for their services. I'm going to do something a little different this time. I'd like to thank all the people with whom I've worked over the years who generously shared their knowledge and experience with me. Without them, I wouldn't be the technician I am today. Without them, this book wouldn't exist. So thanks to all the coworkers in the IT industry, past and present, with whom I have had the honor to work.

Part 1

Troubleshooting Basics

Before I dive right into the meat of this book, I want to get a few basic things out of the way for those readers who might be less experienced in the world of computer service. While this book is primarily targeted at experienced users who simply don't want to commit everything they have to know to memory, it should also be easy to use for someone just getting started. In this chapter, I will cover a basic troubleshooting method, along with some vital tools and utilities all technicians should own. Finally, I'll describe what I think would be the perfect workshop for the computer technician. You know the one I mean? The one none of us will ever get to work in because our bosses are too cheap? Let's get started.

For more information on The CompTIA Trouble-shooting Method, go to page 873, Chapter 35 of *The Complete Guide to A+ Certification.*

A Troubleshooting Method

Scour the books on computer hardware and networking and you'll find as many variations on this theme as there are books. Some of the people who wrote these books are like me and actually worked on computers before they sat down to write a book, and they provide some pretty good approaches. But once you strip away the veneer, all these different approaches boil down to essentially the same basic steps:

- ✔ Identify the problem
- ✔ Re-create the problem
- ✔ Isolate the cause of the problem
- ✔ Decide on a possible solution
- ✔ Test your idea
- ✔ Fix the computer
- ✔ Follow up

Identify the Problem

Step one is always to identify exactly what the customer perceives to be the issue at hand. Sometimes, it is blatantly obvious. When you push the power button, nothing happens. Then again, sometimes getting information out of the user is like getting your toddler to tell you where she hid mommy's magazine.

A few leading questions will usually help you target the real problem. Several of the books I read when I was in training all suggested that the first question you should ask a client is "What changed since the last time it worked?" It took a couple of years for me to figure out that this was a useless question. The answer was always, "Nothing." This demonstrates the difference between an open-ended question and a closed-ended question. A closed-ended question, such as the one above, elicits a response that ends the conversation right there.

You need to be more specific. If the computer still works, but is exhibiting problems, a good question might be, "What were you doing at the moment the problem first appeared?" This represents an open-ended question. The answer provided by the user has a strong potential of leading to other questions. And it may even lead to a solution.

If a specific device, such as a sound card or a modem, is exhibiting peculiarities, you might ask if any new software has been installed, of if another device has been installed on the system. Once in a while, you get lucky and the customer is able to be specific about the problem. That's always a nice head start.

Re-Create the Problem

The next thing you want to do is make the problem happen for you. If you are able to replicate the error or device failure, there might be an error message associated with the problem that can point you in the right direction. Many messages will provide the memory address at which the error occurred and if you can find out what was running at that address, it might give you some ideas. For example, device drivers frequently load to the same memory address each time. Therefore, if the error repeats itself over and over and the address is always the same, it might be a device driver that is generating the error. It could also mean that the RAM stick is bad as well.

In any case, in order to successfully analyze a problem, you need to be able to re-create it. If the problem won't raise its ugly head for you, then the problem might not be with the computer. Technicians cannot so easily fix user errors. However, a good technician can gently point out the errors and show the user how to correct them. A good technician never attempts to demonstrate his or her superiority by making the user feel foolish.

Isolate the Cause of the Problem

This is where the troubleshooting session frequently turns into a turkey shooting session. If the address of the error points to a specific device, you have a head start. If not, you might find yourself resorting to one of the several hardware and software diagnostic tools that I'll discuss later in this Part. The last thing you want to do is to start arbitrarily replacing parts, hoping you'll eventually get lucky. For one thing, that's not a very cost-effective approach, and for another, you run the risk of damaging good parts.

But what if all your diagnostic tools unearth nothing? You've successfully re-created the problem on the computer and now you and your colleagues are standing around scratching your heads and saying, "Never seen anything like that before!" And in this industry, the longer you work at your job, the more likely it is that will happen to you.

That's when it's time to find somebody who has seen the problem before. A good start is online technical support, if you are working on a name brand computer. Most manufacturers maintain an extensive knowledge base. If it's a known problem, they'll be familiar with it.

Even if the computer is a white-box clone made by the Mom and Pop operation that went out of business last year, all hope is not lost. Mom and Pop had to have bought the parts they used somewhere, and those parts came from a manufacturer. Once you've isolated the component that is giving you a hard time, see if you can find anything on the Internet that relates to the problem you're having. Later in this guide, I will be going through the components commonly addressed by technicians, one at a time, and discussing some of the more commonly seen issues and possible solutions.

Decide on a Possible Solution

Now that you think you know what's causing the problem, you probably already have a possible solution in mind. This is your hypothesis. Think about that solution carefully before you implement it. For example, if your solution involves formatting the hard drive, you might want to make sure the customer has backups of any critical data. If he or she doesn't, you might want to think about possible ways of getting that data off before you destroy it permanently.

Also keep in mind that some symptoms are generated by multiple components. Memory errors can be caused by the memory itself, a faulty chipset, or even a bad power supply. Therefore, you need to be thorough in your analysis before you jump into the next step.

Test Your Idea

You think it's a bad CPU, but you're not a hundred-percent certain. If you have another computer lying around that uses a CPU your sick computer will support, you might try installing a known-good CPU in the system. One of the things I do is to keep a collection of "known-goods." These are parts that I can use to test a sick computer. I have several CPUs, at least one example of each of the most commonly used memory sticks, and a couple of motherboards. I keep both an AT and an ATX power supply just for testing purposes.

One thing you probably want to avoid doing is simply ordering in new parts randomly. Distributors are justifiably reluctant to take back opened computer components. They have no way of knowing what precautions you may or may not have taken to protect those components from ESD while they were in your possession. By testing your idea first, you eliminate a lot of unnecessary hassles.

Fix the Computer

Once you're comfortable that your hypothesis is correct and that it fixes the problem, go ahead and implement your solution. Install new parts that the customer can keep and then test the solution. Run the customer's applications for a while. Do your best to replicate the original problem, but keep watching for new problems while you're doing so. It is not at all uncommon for a new problem to appear once the original problem has been fixed. Whatever you do, don't just fire the machine up and say, "This, my friend, is why they pay me the big bucks!" then hand it off to the user. That's a good way of having it come flying back in your face.

Follow Up

You also need to provide customers with proof that you've fixed their problem. And by this, I don't simply mean an invoice that lists what you did and how much it's going to cost them. When they pick up their system, show them it's fixed. Let them poke around on it and try to recreate the original problem themselves. Once they're satisfied the problem has gone away, then you can give them the invoice and watch their eyes glaze over.

Doing this accomplishes two things. First off, you demonstrate to the customer that your solution has worked. That greatly eases the pain of seeing the bill. Second, in the event that the problem reoccurs, you will be able to point out the fact that it was working when it left. While this admittedly does provide a very good method of covering your own bases (in the industry, that's called the CYA solution; don't ask why), it also might be providing some insight into what might be going on over on the customer's side. Is there an environmental issue causing the problem? I once had a computer system that kept coming back with bad power supplies. I finally got on my horse and rode over to the customer's site. I tested the outlet and found that it required immediate attention. You're not supposed to get 140V out of those things!

Just because the computer is now working perfectly doesn't mean your job is done. One of the things they teach you in the military is that no job is complete until the paperwork is done. That holds true of computer repair as well. You need to document exactly what you did. There are some pretty nifty help-desk software solutions that allow you to create a searchable database of problems and their solutions. The larger that database becomes, the more frequently you can simply turn to it for solutions.

The Technician's Toolkit

Contrary to what the salesman at the computer store tries to tell you, the vast majority of the technician's work is done with a very sparse toolkit. In fact, I can't count the number of computers I've fixed with no more than a new part and a Philips screwdriver. Still, there are other tools that, while you don't use them so frequently, when you need one, nothing else will do the trick. If you're going to do this right, invest in the following tools. Some of these tools are illustrated in the accompanying figures.

- ✔ No. 0 and No. 1 Phillips screwdrivers
- ✔ 1/8", 1/4", and 3/16" flat screwdrivers
- ✔ T7, T10, and T15 Torx screwdrivers
- ✔ 3/16" and 1/4" nut drivers
- ✔ 3-claw parts grip
- ✔ Tweezers
- ✔ Chip extractor

- ✔ Chip inserter 14-16 pin ICS
- ✔ Spare parts tube
- ✔ 5" needle nose pliers
- ✔ 8" wire cutter
- ✔ Reverse action tweezers
- ✔ A plastic scribe
- ✔ A small hammer
- ✔ Alcohol-filled cleaning swabs
- ✔ A can of compressed air

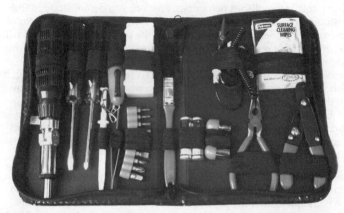

Figure 1.1   A useable toolkit doesn't have to be expensive. This one from Staples set me back thirty bucks and has almost everything I'll ever use in the field. Just one suggestion—lose the reversible screwdriver. The interchangeable tips are a good idea, but get a fixed handle.

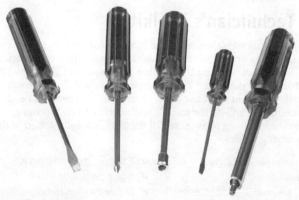

Figure 1.2   For screwdrivers, I use fixed-handle tools for the Philips and flathead, and a fixed handle with interchangeable tips for Torx and other oddball screwheads.

Figure 1.3 Don't even try to work on computers without a set of needle-nosed pliers. You wouldn't believe the number of ways those babies come in handy!

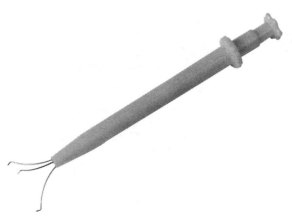

Figure 1.4 A simple little parts gripper is your best friend on those times when the only screw you have that fits the hole just fell between the power supply and the motherboard.

Figure 1.5 Make sure you protect yourself and the equipment you're working on from ESD. A good wrist strap is essential. Just make sure that clip is attached to something that goes to ground. If it isn't, you might as well be wearing a bikini.

A few notes on screwdrivers are in order here. First of all, regardless of what the salesman tells you, always remember a primary commandment to service technicians. Thou Shalt Not Use Magnetized Screwdrivers Near an Integrated Circuit Board! Magnets can damage integrated circuits, such as CPUs, RAM modules, and all those little tiny chips on motherboards and expansion cards. Data can be erased from EEPROMS and disk drives, and microtransistors can be rendered useless. If you drop a screw into the case, you'll discover what the 3-prong parts grip is for.

Second, for a field kit, it is possible to get screwdriver handles with interchangeable tips. These kits drastically reduce the amount of luggage you're carrying around with you. They're not quite as convenient, and I go through about a dozen tips a month from leaving them behind, losing them down into the car seat, and dropping them into the snow. For a portable kit, interchangeable tips are acceptable. For a permanent workshop, I strongly recommend complete screwdriver sets.

There are also a few optional tools that you will find very handy if you can afford to add them to your arsenal. If money is an issue (and when isn't it?), these aren't used often enough to worry about from the start.

For more information on Hardware-Based Troubleshooting Tools, go to page 875, Chapter 35 of *The Complete Guide to A+ Certification*.

However, as you gain experience, you'll find more and more reasons to use them. These tools include:

✔ Serial port loopback adapter
✔ Parallel port loopback adapter
✔ A good multimeter
✔ A cable tester
✔ A POST card
✔ An antistatic vacuum cleaner

Loopback Adapters

Testing a port can sometimes be a matter of having that port talk to itself. By doing this, you are verifying the functionality of the port itself and taking external variables, such as device drivers or cables, out of the equation. In order to do that, you'll need a specialized plug called a loopback adapter that wraps the signal back to the computer rather than sending it out to a device. This takes the device out of the loop and tells you whether or not it is the port that is bad rather than a device or cable. Loopback adapters are available for either serial ports or parallel ports (**Figure 1.6**).

Figure 1.6 Loopback adapters help you diagnose problems with the serial and parallel ports on a machine.

The Multimeter

Sometimes simply testing for power or continuity can tell you a lot
about what's going on. A simple and inexpensive tool for that is a multimeter. The multimeter will tell you if you have proper power coming
out of the connectors coming from your power supply. You can use it to
test a wire for continuity. It's also useful for testing those ceramic fuses
that don't let you see the wire. I recommend that you spend a few extra
bucks on this and get a digital version (shown in **Figure 1.7**). They're
easier to work with.

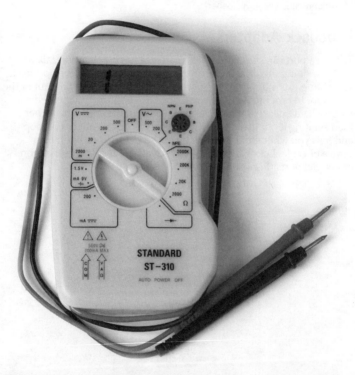

Figure 1.7 Buy a digital multimeter. It'll save you lots and lots of headaches.

The POST Card

Unfortunately, this is not the one you send to your mother-in-law
when you go on vacation. These are a bit expensive for that. The POST

card I'm talking about is used to diagnose problems that occur during the boot process that prevent the computer from starting properly. It mounts into an empty expansion slot, and while the computer is booting (or trying to, anyway), it's zipping off light patterns on an LED readout so fast that you can't possibly read them. Don't worry about that. The ones you can't read are the ones you don't care about. They represent components that passed.

At the point that the boot process fails, the readout will display a pattern of lights that represents a specific component. The POST card ships with a booklet that itemizes all of those error messages. All you have to do is look up the number displayed, and it tells you what part of the POST process failed. JDR Microdevices, in San Jose, California, offers four different options. They have standard POST cards in both PCI and ISA form. But they also have ISA and PCI versions that test the BIOS as well as the POST process.

A more advanced version of this card is available from Ultra-X, Inc. in Santa Clara, California. It can go beyond the POST test (which it does rather extensively) and continue to test RAM, drive operation including CD-ROM drives, and much more. The Professional Kit includes an impressive array of diagnostics software utilities, a collection of loopback plugs, and the PCI card. This is the card illustrated in **Figure** 1.8. A rather interesting option, offered by PCWiz out of Clearwater, Florida, offers a single card that has an ISA connector on one edge and a PCI connector on other.

Figure 1.8 This POST card, by Ultra-X, is one of the most formidable tools you can have in your arsenal. It identifies problems that occur during the POST process.

Cable Testers

Cable testers are good for checking RJ-45 network cables. They come in a wide variety of shapes and sizes, but they basically boil down to one of two types. A standard cable tester can check for continuity and also tell you which pin on one side of the cable is leading to which pin on the other side. Advanced cable testers not only detect a break, but also tell you how far down the cable from the tester the break occurs. This greatly enhances your ability to fix the problem.

The cable tester may or may not come with a remote unit. If it doesn't, there will be two sockets on the tester for plugging both ends of the cable into. These can be of limited use when you are testing an installed cable. A cable tester with a remote unit provides a second, smaller unit that can be plugged onto the cable at the user's end. Then, from the hub or patch panel, you can perform your tests.

Troubleshooting Software

Troubleshooting software for the professional technician is just as essential as a decent set of screwdrivers. Most of us consider the software to be the most significant weapon in our arsenal. With the right software, you can pinpoint a problem in a few minutes instead of spending hours and hours using trial-and-error methodology.

For more information on Software Troubleshooting Essentials, go to page 878, Chapter 35 of *The Complete Guide to A+ Certification*.

A good technician carries a few different utilities. Some people favor integrated suites of utilities, such as those offered by Norton and PC Tools (and others). Others tend to collect their own favorites. I'm one of the latter. Another thing that I've discovered is that you really don't have to spend a fortune on software utilities. For example, if you purchase the Ultra-X POST card, you can buy it with a bundle of very powerful software tools. Even if you don't have that kind of money to throw around, there are dozens of free utilities on the Internet that you can download. In addition to the free ones (which are generally either very specific, or very limited in scope), there are some shareware utilities that, if you pay the registration fee, can compete with the best of the commercial suites. I maintain a collection of free and shareware utilities on my Web site at www.mwgraves.com, along with shortcuts to companies that provide discounts on commercial suites and the hardware tools I listed above.

I would like to summarize some of the available software tools below. This is far from being an all-inclusive list. To attempt that amazing feat would require a book far too thick to carry around in the field, and I would die of old age long before I finished it.

Commercial Troubleshooting Suites

✔ Ultra-X QuickTech Professional (www.uxd.com)
✔ PC Diagnostics (www.pc-diagnostics.com)
✔ Norton Systemworks—Includes software diagnostics as well
   (www.symantec.com/sabu/sysworks/basic)
✔ Micro2000 (www.micro2000.com/toolkit/index.php)

Shareware Troubleshooting Utilities

✔ TuffTest Professional—HIGHLY recommended!
   (www.tufftest.com/ttp01.htm)
✔ Sisoft Sandra—Available in four different versions, ranging from an
   inexpensive personal version to an enterprise version that would pay for
   a decent car (www.sisoftware.net)

Freeware Troubleshooting Utilities

✔ Fresh Utilities (www.freshdevices.com)
✔ CPUID (www.mwgraves.com)
✔ CMOS Backup (www.mwgraves.com)
✔ MemTest (www.mwgraves.com)
✔ Sound Card Detector (www.mwgraves.com)

Setting Up Shop

For many people, the ultimate goal of certification is simply to find a
better job and jumpstart their careers. There is absolutely nothing
wrong with that. My deepest respect goes out to people who look
around and realize that life could be better and that it is in their power
to make it better. However, people who work for other people are
pretty much at the mercy of whatever environment that employer
provides.

Other people aspire to be self-employed. The old nine-to-five grind just
isn't their cup of cappuccino. Being in control of their own destinies is
the only thing that will make them happy. If I were to take exception to
that philosophy, I'd have to stop writing these books and get a real job.

A professional repair shop properly designed and in a good location
can be a lucrative enterprise. But such an enterprise doesn't design
itself. If you are just getting started, now is the time to do it right the
first time. I've worked in really spiffy shops and I've worked in a few
that my wife's cat could have done a better job of designing.

To do this right, there are a few variables to take into consideration:

✔ Comfort and productivity
✔ Lighting
✔ Electrical power
✔ Antistatic protection
✔ Customer access (and lack thereof)

Comfort

If this is going to be your full-time gig, the last thing you want is to make it a miserable place to work. Therefore, you need a workstation designed around your personal requirements. You need to be able to sit high over a computer to be able to peer down into the case. On the other hand, you don't want back fatigue to set in. A good workbench provides ready access to the tools you need without requiring you to jump up and run all over the shop every time you need something.

Workbenches with high stools, preferably the type with backrests, are ideal for most people. Someone who needs wheelchair access will need the bench designed around that aspect of his or her life. Pegboards with hangers for the various tools you use on a day-to-day basis can be placed either along the wall behind the bench, or, if you have more than one workbench in your shop, dividers between the benches can be pegboard equipped and the tools will be easier to reach.

Air conditioning is critical. That may sound like an extravagance to some. But the first time you pay to replace a customer's motherboard out of your own pocket because sweat dripping from your face caused sparks to fly, you'll take a whole new approach to creature comforts.

When you need a break, it will be exceedingly convenient to have a separate table set up for having a cup of English Breakfast and a scone. The last place in the world you want to be eating or drinking is at your workbench. See the above statement about dripping sweat and you should be able to make the transition.

You'll also need easy access to restroom facilities. After all, even computer technicians are human. When nature calls, they will answer. One way or the other.

Lighting

Nothing is harder on the eyes than straining to see something tiny in poor light. General lighting in the work area needs to be sufficiently bright without being blinding. At each workbench, you need some form of adjustable lamp that can be positioned to point light in a specific direction. That way you can see into the computer case without trying to hold a flashlight between your teeth, enabling you to attach a CPU fan and not drool onto the motherboard at the same time.

Electrical Power

It goes without saying that if you plan on plugging something in, you need an outlet. However, as a professional technician, you have a few more specific requirements. For one thing, you'll need more power, and you'll need cleaner power than the average spare bedroom has. Each workbench should be equipped with a minimum of two 110V grounded AC outlets.

Remember that while you have your customer's computer in your possession, you are responsible for its safety. I'm not a lawyer and this isn't a book about law, but if you do your homework, you will find that most states protect the customer over the business owner. In many states, it doesn't matter how many signs you post that say you're not responsible for a customer's property; you are. Therefore, I strongly recommend that you put professional quality surge suppressors at each workstation for your customers' equipment. You'll be glad you did.

Antistatic Protection

You need to be protecting your customers' equipment from static electricity as well. As I've emphasized over and over again in my previous books, static electricity is a computer's worst enemy. A spark you can't even see or feel can destroy a CPU or an IC on a component board.

A well-designed bench will have two different antistatic mats. One will be positioned on the floor to absorb electrostatic discharge (ESD) that is generated by the chair rolling back and forth. Without such a mat, all that static electricity flows into your body and you become a living, breathing capacitor. The second goes on the bench and this is where you put the computer you're working on.

The antistatic mats I'm talking about here aren't the ones you see at office supply stores. While those may do a reasonable job of resisting ESD accumulation, they do nothing to dissipate it. A professional antistatic mat draws the charge away from the work area and sends it to the ground in your building's electrical system. A company called ESD Systems, Inc. specializes in these products and you might be surprised at how little it will cost to protect yourself from a lawsuit.

In addition to antistatic mats for the floor and bench area, each technician should be required to wear antistatic wristbands. Just wearing
them isn't enough. Like the mats, they have to go to ground somewhere, or they are accomplishing nothing. If you're not working on the
power supply, you can simply keep the computer plugged into the wall
and clip the wrist strap to the metal frame of the enclosure. If you are
working on the power supply, obviously that's not a good idea. Clip the
lead to something that you know goes to ground.

Finally, one of the jobs you'll find yourself doing time and again is
cleaning the dust out of systems that have been sitting in somebody's
corner for months or even years. The way most systems are designed,
cool air brought in from the outside by the cooling fans is not filtered.
Dust accumulates rapidly. Some of the systems I've worked on should
be declared environmental hazard areas!

Most technicians reach for a can of compressed air and blow it out.
Admittedly, this is better than nothing. But a better approach is to not
blow the dust off the motherboard and into your CD-ROM or floppy
disk drive. A good vacuum cleaner is a sound investment. However,
specialized vacuum cleaners are required for the service bench. A
cleaner you buy at the department store sucks just fine. But the plastic
nozzle generates enough static to kill a dozen computers per second.
Menda is one of several companies that manufacture ESD-safe vacuum
cleaners for the workshop. I strongly recommend that this not be an
optional item, but a required investment.

Customer Access

If you're going to run a business, you need to attract customers. If customers find your shop difficult to locate, or if parking is non-existent,
they'll find another technician with whom they can do business. There
is nothing wrong with operating out of your home if you have the
space for the shop and adequate parking. But a few considerations are
in order.

You want customers to access the service counter as easily as possible.
If you're working out of your house, you don't want them traipsing
through your living room to get there. A dedicated customer entrance is
a must. They'll be carrying heavy computers in their arms when they
come in, so you want doors that open inward. You can help them with
the door on their way out.

Once they get there, where are they going to set the computer? On that tiny six-inch strip of maple or pine that separates the top half from the bottom on your divided door? You're going to want a bench or table for them to set it down. If you're going to do this right, equip that bench with an electrical outlet and a keyboard, monitor, and mouse so you can fire up their system (if possible) and have customers demonstrate their problems without dragging them back into your service area.

In general, it's a bad idea to give customers unrestricted access to the shop. They aren't protected against static electricity, so anything they happen to touch is at risk. And quite frankly, you don't know many of these people from Moses. How do you know if they've got sticky fingers or not?

Conclusion

Okay, now that the basics are out of the way, it's time for you to get to work. My apologies, but this is the only chapter where you get to read my elegant prose. The rest of the book will consist of tables, lists, charts, diagrams, and photographs that will help you fix computers. Only where necessary will I intervene with personal commentary. Go to my other books for that.

Part 2

Getting the System on the Bench

General computer problems break down into two umbrella categories. Either the system won't boot at all, or it boots and then doesn't work right. Either one of these situations can be caused either by hardware or by software. In this Part, I'll start with the system that won't boot at all. For information about the system that boots but doesn't work correctly, see all the rest of this book. The system that doesn't boot falls into one of three varieties:

✔ You push the button and nothing happens.
✔ You push the button, the system starts to power up and emits a bunch of beeps, and then dies.
✔ You push the button, the system spews out one or more messages, and then dies.

The following sections contain guidelines for each of the aforementioned situations.

The Initial Diagnosis

When troubleshooting a system that won't boot, always try unplugging all ribbon cables and removing memory sticks and all expansion cards.

For more information on Troubleshooting Roadmaps, go to page 880, Chapter 35 of *The Complete Guide to A+ Certification.*
Boot the machine. You should get the correct beep codes your version of BIOS issues when it detects no memory.

1. Did you get the beep codes? Yes, move on to the next step. No? It's a bad CPU. Try a known good one.
2. If you get the beeps, next insert the memory sticks, one at a time, rebooting after each one. If you can install all memory with no memory-related beep codes, move on to Step 3. If not, replace the memory.
3. Now add the video card. If the video card is good, you'll start seeing the boot sequence on the monitor. If not, you'll hear the beep codes for a bad video card.
4. Now add the floppy diskette drive cable. It's pretty rare that the floppy drive prevents a system from booting, but to be consistent, start the machine again. There should be no difference from when you booted to good RAM.
5. Add the IDE cables, one at a time, rebooting after each one, starting with the hard disk cable. Quite often, a hard disk failure won't elicit beeps, even with a BIOS with beep codes programmed in for a hard disk failure. But the machine might simply come screeching to a halt. If this happens, or if you get beep codes indicating a failure, use the same cable to plug in the CD-ROM, assuming one is installed. If you get no error codes with the CD-ROM, replace the hard disk drive. If you get exactly the same error with the CD-ROM, your problem is either with cable or the motherboard. If this happens, go to Step 5. If you have no error code with the hard disk or the CD-ROM, skip to Step 6.
6. Assuming the failure followed over to the CD-ROM, always try the easiest thing first. Swap out the IDE cable. Still got a problem? Swap out the motherboard.
7. Now add the expansion cards. Add them one at a time, restarting the machine at each reboot. Most expansion cards won't have beep codes, and many don't elicit text error messages. When the system locks, you'll know you have the culprit.
8. If all of the above failed to reveal the problem, look up the tech support number for the manufacturer and give them a call. You did your part.

Here are some questions you might get asked by customers whose computers won't boot.

✔ **My machine fails to boot and returns a bunch of beeps. What do they mean?** It means that you need to skip over to Part 3 and read the Diagnosing Beep Codes section.

✔ **I'm trying to boot my machine, but it tells me about an "Invalid Checksum" and hangs.** Your CMOS settings went south for the winter on you. Perhaps the battery went dead, or maybe you took a voltage hit and are lucky your system isn't totally fried. Either way, you can usually run the BIOS setup program from boot and reset the configuration to Factory Defaults. This will get the system up and running and you can tweak the settings either now or later.

✔ **Okay, wise guy. I went to try that, but my computer won't tell me what buttons to push to get into the CMOS setup. What now?** I can only say, "Been there, done that." Sometimes the brandname computers don't provide an opening screen telling you where to go. If they've got a

> For more information on The Programs of ROM BIOS, go to page 118, Chapter 6 of *The Complete Guide to A+ Certification.*

flash screen advertising a product you've already bought, try hitting the ESC key. That will usually clear the flash screen and you'll see POST messages. This might possibly tell you how to enter setup. If that doesn't work, try one of the key sequences listed in Part 3, in the BIOS Configuration section.

✔ **None of these work!** Yeah, well, that's why manufacturers have technical support. Give them a call, or better yet, check their Web site. That's usually faster.

✔ **Oh, no! I made some settings to my CMOS and now my system won't boot!** Let that be a lesson to you. Don't ever change more than one parameter at a time. Wait till you see what affect that has before you make other changes. In this case, simply reset the system back to factory defaults and start over from scratch.

✔ **Every time I boot my machine it tells me that it's "Updating the ESCD" even though I didn't add any new devices.** The ESCD is your extended system configuration data, and on Plug 'n Play machines it tells the BIOS how to configure the devices. If you have an OS that is Plug 'n Play, such as Windows 95 or later, it might disagree with your BIOS

> For more information on Troubleshooting BIOS, go to page 124, Chapter 6 of *The Complete Guide to A+ Certification.*

about how to configure the settings. In most cases, it can do this without any problems, and the BIOS accepts and remembers the changes. In some cases, however, the ESCD isn't permanently changed, but the device configuration was. So the BIOS resets the device on boot up. Windows sees this and say's "Hey, I'm the boss around here," and once again resets the configuration. And on and on it goes, a never-ending cycle. It isn't hurting anything, so you can simply ignore it. On the other hand, if it is annoying you to no end, you might see if your manufacturer supplies a BIOS upgrade to your computer. On some early Pentium machines (and just about anything made prior to that), that will involve replacing the BIOS chip. If your BIOS is flashable, you can burn the new code to your BIOS chip.

✔ **Thanks for the tip buddy! I just flashed my BIOS and now my system is an oversized doorstop!** One of two things happened here. You either chose, or were supplied, the wrong version of BIOS for your particular motherboard, or you downloaded the software from the Internet and got a corrupt download. If your computer is relatively recent, it will include a feature called boot block. When a computer with boot block encounters corrupted BIOS, it automatically checks the floppy for a new version to flash. Yet one more reason not to retire your floppy diskette drive! Get a correct or clean version, pop it in the floppy drive, and restart. You're back up and running. If your machine does not support boot block, then pray that you have a removable BIOS chip. Better yet, only purchase motherboards that do feature removable BIOS. You can order in a new chip from the manufacturer. (That'll be fifty bucks please. Will that be MasterCard or Visa?) If the BIOS is soldered on, why don't you see what is new in the world of CPUs while you're shopping for your new mother-board? And by the way—it wasn't my fault. I only told you what to do. I didn't download the flash for you!

✔ **Somebody entered a password on one of the computers in our office and now nobody can access the system.** It's hard to get good help these days, isn't it? All is not lost. Many motherboards have a jumper for disconnecting the onboard battery from the CMOS chip. After a couple of minutes, put the jumper back on. Your BIOS settings will be back to factory defaults and you're good to go. If you can't find a jumper that does this, or aren't sure which one, just pull the battery out. Don't get any fingerprints on the battery, though. That will shorten the life of the battery by a large margin.

For more information on Troubleshooting Memory, go to page 195, Chapter 9 of *The Complete Guide to A+ Certification*.

For more information on Troubleshooting the Expansion Bus, go to page 233, Chapter 10 of *The Complete Guide to A+ Certification*.

For more information on Troubleshooting Hard Drives, go to page 340, Chapter 14 of *The Complete Guide to A+ Certification*.

You Push the Button and Nothing Happens

Before You Open the Case...

✔ Are you plugged in? Computers don't run without juice. Make sure there are no loose connections.

✔ Are you plugged into a surge suppressor? (I certainly hope so.) Make sure it is plugged in and turned on. And while this may sound like a no-brainer, check to make sure it isn't plugged into itself. Twice (not just once, but twice), I've gone on site to a "dead" computer and found the power strip looped back to itself.

✔ Is the switch on your power supply set to the correct voltage? In the U.S., is should be set to 110–115V (**Figure 2.1**). Overseas, it should be set to 220. The system won't power if incorrectly set.

Figure 2.1 There is a switch on the back of your power supply to select what country's voltage to use. Make sure it's set correctly.

Open the Case

✔ Do you see an LED glowing? Many system boards have a Power Good LED to indicate that the board is getting power. If it is glowing, the power supply is working.

✔ Is the 20-pin connector from the power supply firmly seated into the motherboard? Since this connector is two rows of 10 connectors, it is often called the 2×10 connector.

✔ Is the wire from the power switch on the front of the case properly seated on the motherboard?

✔ On Pentium 4 machines, there is a separate power connector for the

> For more information on AT, ATX, and SFX Power Supplies, go to page 84, Chapter 4 of *The Complete Guide to A+ Certification*.

> For more information on Troubleshooting Power Supplies, go to page 84, Chapter 4 of *The Complete Guide to A+ Certification*.

CPU. This is the processor core voltage supply connector and it consists of two rows of two pins. It is often called the ATX12 connector. Is it hooked up? Failure to connect that has been known to damage motherboards.

✔ Is the power supply delivering power to the motherboard? Check the 20-pin connection from the power supply. The illustration in **Figure 2.2** and **Table 2.1** indicate proper readings.

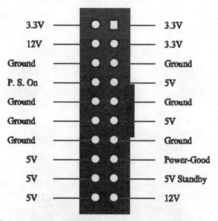

Figure 2.2 If the power supply is good, you should be able to get power readings from the 2×10 connector.

ATX Power Supply Connector Specifications

Pin #	Signal	Color	Pin #	Signal	Color
1	+3.3V	Orange	11	+3.3V	Orange
2	+3.3V	Orange	12	-12V	Blue
3	Ground	Black	13	Ground	Black
4	+5V	Red	14	Power Switch On	Green
5	Ground	Black	15	Ground	Ground
6	+5V	Red	16	Ground	Ground

Pin #	Signal	Color	Pin #	Signal	Color
7	Ground	Black	17	Ground	Black
8	Power Good	Gray	18	-5V	White
9	+5V Standby	Purple	19	+5V	Red
10	+12V	Yellow	20	+5V	Red

Table 2.1: Proper signal readings and color codes for an ATX power supply connector.

✔ Are you getting power from the power supply? Use your multimeter to check voltage on one of the free Molex connectors. This connector consists of one row of four connectors. If there is no current, you most likely have a bad power supply. **Figure 2.5** and **Table 2.2** show the proper readings for a standard Molex connector.

✔ On a Pentium 4 machine, does the ATX12 connector deliver power to the CPU? **Figure 2.6** and **Table 2.3** list the proper power readings for the ATX12.

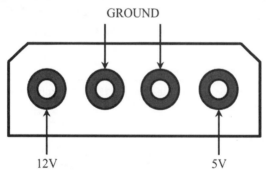

Figure 2.3   The appropriate power readings for the Molex connectors.

Molex Connector Specifications

Pin #	Voltage	Color
1	+12V	Yellow
2	Ground	Black
3	Ground	Black
4	+5V	Red

Table 2.2: Power readings and color codes for a Molex connector.

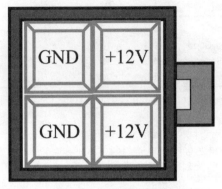

Figure 2.4 The appropriate power readings for the ATX12 connector on a P4 machine.

P4 ATX12 Connector Specifications

Pin #	Voltage	Color	Pin #	Voltage	Color
1	Ground	Black	3	+12V	Yellow
2	Ground	Black	4	+12V	Yellow

Table 2.3: Appropriate power readings for 12V ATX12 connector on a P4 power supply.

> **NOTE:** A power supply specifically designed for a Pentium 4 machine, as noted in the text, will have a separate ATX12 12V power connector to power the core voltage power supply for the processor. These power supplies are designated ATX12V. Intel and most power supply manufacturers note in their specifications that failing to hook the connection up may damage the motherboard, the power supply, or both. While this is true of a P4 MB/PS combination, it is perfectly safe to use the ATX12V power supply on an earlier Pentium II or Pentium III machine. Just tie the ATX12 12V cable out of the way.

Part 3

Motherboard Components

The following sections deal with the motherboard and various components that reside on the motherboard. Identifying and troubleshooting these components are among the more challenging tasks a technician will face. Over the next few pages I will provide a tour of the various components of the motherboard, including the sockets and the cables that attach to the motherboard.

Managing Resources

The key thing to remember when troubleshooting all devices is that each device needs to be recognized by the system as a unique entity. If two devices appear to be the same, one of them is going to get ignored. There are four major configurations settings used by devices to get recognized:

✔ Interrupt Request (IRQ) lines
✔ I/O addresses
✔ Direct Memory Access (DMA) channels
✔ COM and LPT ports

With modern operating systems, IRQs can generally be shared. There are a couple of exceptions to this rule, but the OS knows how to handle those exceptions. I/O addresses can **never** be shared under any set of circumstances. Neither can DMA channels. With only a couple of exceptions, all devices require an IRQ. The two exceptions are joysticks and some video cards. **All** devices require an I/O address, and only a few devices make use of DMA channels. Floppy disk drives, sound cards, and parallel ports configured to use the Extended Capabilities Port (ECP) all use DMA channels.

IRQs

From a hardware standpoint, there are fifteen available IRQ channels.

For more information on Interrupt Request Lines, go to page 206, Chapter 10 of *The Complete Guide to A+ Certification*.

Since the early days of the PC, certain IRQs have been assigned to specific functions. **Table 3.1** lists the IRQs and their general usage.

IRQ Usage

IRQ #	Assigned Device
0	System Timer
1	Keyboard Controller
2	Cascade to IRQ 9 - Not Available
3	Com Port 2
4	Com Port 1
5	LPT 2
6	Floppy Disk Controller
7	LPT 1
8	Real-Time Clock
9	Available
10	Available
11	Available
12	Available
13	Math Coprocessor
14	Primary IDE Controller
15	Secondary IDE Controller

Table 3.1: Conventional IRQ usage as handed down through the ages

Another thing to remember is that IRQs are assigned priorities. The lower the IRQ number, the higher the priority. **Figure 3.1** shows a listing of the IRQs and their priorities.

Windows 2000 and later are capable of using virtual IRQs. These are arbitrary IRQ assignments handed out by the OS that get translated into the actual hardware assignment. Therefore, don't be surprised to find a device on IRQ17. But don't go looking for IRQ17 in the CMOS setup either. It won't exist.

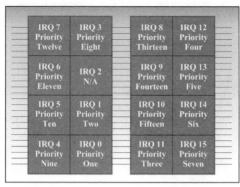

IRQ 7 Priority Twelve	IRQ 3 Priority Eight	IRQ 8 Priority Thirteen	IRQ 12 Priority Four
IRQ 6 Priority Eleven	IRQ 2 N/A	IRQ 9 Priority Fourteen	IRQ 13 Priority Five
IRQ 5 Priority Ten	IRQ 1 Priority Two	IRQ 10 Priority Fifteen	IRQ 14 Priority Six
IRQ 4 Priority Nine	IRQ 0 Priority One	IRQ 11 Priority Three	IRQ 15 Priority Seven

Figure 3.1 IRQs in a system have priorities. If you want a particular device to have a slight advantage in bus access, make sure it has an IRQ with a higher priority.

I/O Addresses

The I/O address is what the CPU actually uses to locate a specific device. Therefore, there can be no duplication and there can be no overlap of I/O addresses. That results in an irresolvable conflict, and the second device scanned during POST will be ignored. I/O addresses are carefully managed in order to prevent conflict. **Table 3.2** lists commonly used I/O addresses and their usages.

For more information on Input Output Addresses, go to page 208, Chapter 10 of *The Complete Guide to A+ Certification*.

Common I/O Address Assignments

Address	Usage
000-00Fh	DMA controller, channels 0 to 3
010-01Fh	(System use)
020-023h	Interrupt controller #1 (020-021h)
024-02Fh	(System use)
030-03Fh	(System use)
040-043h	System timer
044-04Fh	(System use)
050-05Fh	(System use)
060-063h	Keyboard & PS/2 mouse (060h), Speaker (061h)
064-067h	Keyboard & PS/2 mouse (064h)
068-06Fh	Free to use

continues

Common I/O Address Assignments (*continued*)

Address	Usage
070-073h	Real-time clock/CMOS, (Nonmaskable interrupt - 070-071h)
074-07Fh	(System use)
080-083h	DMA page register 0-2
084h	DMA page register 3
089-08Bh	DMA page register 4-6
08Fh	DMA page register 7
090-09Fh	(System use)
0A0-0A3h	Interrupt controller #2
0A4-0BFh	(System use)
0C0-0CFh	DMA controller, channels 4-7 (0C0-0DFh, bytes 1-16)
0D0-0DFh	DMA controller, channels 4-7 (0C0-0DFh, bytes 17-32)
0E0-0EFh	(System use)
0F0-0FFh	Floating point unit (FPU/NPU/Math coprocessor)
100-12Fh	(System use)
130-15Fh	Commonly used for SCSI controllers
160-167h	Free to use
168-16Fh	Quaternary IDE controller, master drive
170-077h	Secondary IDE controller, master drive
178-1E7h	Free to use
1E8-1EFh	Tertiary IDE controller, master drive
1F0-1F7h	Primary IDE controller, master drive
1F8-1FFh	Free to use
200-207h	Joystick controller
208-20Bh	Free to use
20B-20Fh	(System use)
210-21Fh	Free to use
220-22Fh	Sound card
230-23Fh	Some SCSI adapters
240-24Fh	Some sound cards, some SCSI adapters, some NE2000 network cards
250-25Fh	Some NE2000 network cards
260-26Fh	Some NE2000 network cards, some non-NE2000 network cards, some sound cards
270-273h	(System use)
274-278H	Plug 'n Play system devices
279-27Fh	LPT2
280-28Fh	Some sound cards, some NE2000 network cards
290-29Fh	Some NE2000 network cards
2C0-2E7h	Free to use

Address	Usage
2E8-2EFh	COM port 4
2F0-2F7h	Free to use
2F8-2FFh	COM port 2
300-301h	MIDI port
300-30Fh	Some NE2000 network cards
310-31Fh	Some NE2000 network cards
320-323h	Some non-NE2000 network cards
320-32Fh	Some NE2000 network cards
320-327h	PC-XT hard disk controller
330-333h	MIDI port
330-33Fh	Some NE2000 network cards, some SCSI controllers
340-34Fh	Some SCSI controllers
350-35Fh	Some NE2000 network cards, some SCSI controllers
360-363h	Some tape backup controller cards
360-36Fh	Some NE2000 network cards
370-373h	Some tape backup controller cards
370-37Fh	Some NE2000 network cards
378-37Fh	LPT1 (or LPT2 on monochrome systems)
380-387h	Free to use
388-38Bh	FM synthesizer
38C-3AFh	Free to use
3B0-3BBh	VGA or monochrome video
3BC-3BFh	LPT1 on monochrome systems
3C0-3CFh	VGA or CGA video
3D3-3DFh	VGA or EGO video
3E0-3E3h	Some tape backup controllers
3E8-3Efh	COM port 3
3EC-3Efh	Tertiary IDE controller
3F0-3F7h	Floppy disk controller
3F8-3FFh	COM port 1
3f6-3F7h	Primary IDE

Table 3.2: While it may appear on this table that some devices overlap in their I/O address range, in fact, this is not possible. These indicate devices that may potentially occupy the range. If one device already possesses that I/O address, no other device may share it.

DMA Channels

DMA channels mattered much more in the old days than they do today. Today's faster expansion busses allow direct access to memory without using special tricks. However, for compatibility purposes, DMA is still alive and well, and a conflict can result in a device not working. For example, if you have a sound card using DMA3 and you configure your parallel port to use ECP—and tell it to use DMA3—when you reboot your system, everything will work fine as long as you don't try to

For more information on Direct Memory Access Channels, go to page 212, Chapter 10 of *The Complete Guide to A+ Certification.*

play Stravinsky and print the manuscript for your pocket guide at the same time. If you do, your system will lock up like a tombstone.

To give you an idea of how archaic the idea of DMA usage really is, consider that there are 8-bit channels and 16-bit channels. This is very useful in a day of 64-bit computing, isn't it? Common DMA usage is listed in **Table 3.3**.

DMA Channel Usage

8-bit Channels

Channel	Usage
DMA0	Memory refresh
DMA1	Available
DMA2	Floppy disk drive
DMA3	Available

16-bit Channels

Channel	Usage
DMA4	Cascade
DMA5	Available
DMA6	Available
DMA7	Available

Table 3.3: There are still devices manufactured today that require DMA channels to be configured.

COM and LPT Ports

On the back of your computer are places to plug in serial devices, such as an external modem, and other places to plug in parallel devices, such

For more information on COM and LPT Ports, go to page 213, Chapter 10 of *The Complete Guide to A+ Certification.*

as a printer. Contrary to the way some manufacturers choose to label these ports, these are not your COM or LPT ports. These are your serial and parallel ports. Serial and parallel ports are physical sockets in which to plug cables.

COM and LPT ports are logical ports. They consist of preconfigured combinations of IRQ and I/O addresses. To emphasize why this difference is important to understand, consider this. A serial port can be configured to use any one of the available COM ports. Likewise, a parallel port might be configured to use any of the LPT ports. They are not locked into one another. The COM and LPT ports are listed in **Table 3.4**.

COM and LPT Port Assignments

Port Name	IRQ	I/O
COM1	4	3F8h
COM2	3	2F8h
COM3	4	3E8h
COM4	3	2E8h
LPT1	7	378h
LPT2	5	278h

Table 3.4: Common LPT and COM port assignments

Motherboard Components

Key components you need to be able to identify include CPU sockets and slots, memory slots, and the various cables that connect to the

For more information on Understanding CPUs, go to page 133, Chapter 7 of *The Complete Guide to A+ Certification*.

motherboard. To make this easier to read, I'll simply include the CPU socket in a table (**Table 3.5** and **Figure 3.2**).

CPU Slots and Sockets

CPU Sockets and Slots: Past, Present, and Future

Socket/Slot	# Pins	Voltage	Multiplier variations	CPUs supported
486 Socket	168	5v	1.0x, 2.0x, 3.0x	80486DX, 80486DX2, 80486DX4
Socket 1	169	5v	1.0x, 2.0x,3.0x	80486DX, 80486DX2, 80486DX4, 80486SX

continues

CPU Sockets and Slots, Past, Present, and Future (*continued*)

Socket/Slot	# Pins	Voltage	Multiplier variations	CPUs supported
Socket 2	238	5v	1.0x, 2.0x, 3.0x	80486DX, 80486DX2, 80486DX4, 80486SX
Socket 3	237 ZIF	3.3v 5v	1.0x, 2.0x, 3.0x	80486DX, 80486DX2, 80486DX4, 80486SX
Socket 4	273 ZIF	5v	none	Pentium
Socket 5	296 ZIF	STD VR VRE	1.5x, 2.0x	Pentium
Socket 6	235 ZIF	3.3v	2.0x, 3.0x	80486DX4
Socket 7	321 ZIF	Split STD VR VRE VRT	1.5x, 1.75x, 2.0x 2.33x, 2.5x, 2.66x 3.0x, 3.33x, 3.5x 4.0x, 4.5x, 5.0x 5.5x, 6.0x	Pentium, K5, K6, 6x86
Socket 8	387 ZIF	VID VRM (2.1v~3.5v)	2.0x, 2.5x, 3.0x 4.5x, 5.0x, 5.5x 6.0x, 6.5x, 7.0x 7.5x, 8.0x	Pentium Pro
Socket 370	370 ZIF	VID VRM (1.3v~2.1v)	4.5x, 5.0x, 5.5x 6.0x, 6.5x, 7.0x 7.5x, 8.0x	Celeron, Pentium III
Socket 423	423 ZIF	VID VRM	13.0x, 14.0x, 15.0x, 16.0x, 17.0x, 18.0x, 19.0x, 20.0x	Intel P4 Willamette, Northwood, and Celeron Willamette
Socket 478	478 ZIF	VID VRM	15.0x, 16.0x, 17.0x, 18.0x, 19.0x, 20.0x, 22.0x, 24.0x, 25.0x, 26.0x	Intel P4 Willamette, Northwood, Prescott, and Celeron Willamette and Northwood
Socket 603/604	603/602 ZIF	VID VRM	14.0x, 15.0x, 17.0x, 18.0x, 20.0x, 22.0x	Intel Foster, Prestonia, Nocona, Gallatin

Socket/Slot	# Pins	Voltage	Multiplier variations	CPUs supported
Socket 754	754 ZIF	VID VRM	4x, 5x, 6x, 7x	Athlon Clawhammer, San Diego
Socket 940	940 ZIF	VID VRM	Not Available	Opteron, Sledge-hammer
PAC418	418 VLIF	VID VRM	5.5x. 6.0x	Intel Merced
PAC611	611 VLIF	VID VRM	4.5X, 5.0X	Intel McKinley, Madison, Deerfield, Montecito, Shavano
Socket A	462	VID VRM (1.3v~2.05v)	6.0x, 6.5x, 7.0x 7.5x, 8.0x	Athlon, Duron
Slot A	242	VID VRM (1.3v~2.05v)	5.0x, 5.5x, 6.0x 6.5x, 7.0x, 7.5x 8.0x	Athlon
Slot 1	242	VID VRM (1.3v~3.3v)	3.5x, 4.0x, 4.5x 5.0x, 5.5x, 6.0x 6.5x	Celeron, Pentium Pro, Pentium II, Pentium III
Slot 2	330	VID VRM (1.3v~3.3v)	4.0x, 4.5x, 5.0x 5.5x, 6.0x	Xeon

Table 3.5: An overview of different CPU sockets and slots

Figure 3.2 This motherboard is particularly useful for illustration purposes because it has a Slot 1 CPU socket sitting right next to a Socket 370. Don't get too excited, though. It's not a dual-CPU board; you can only use one socket or the other

Memory Slots

Memory sockets on any system boards seen today will be some variation of the DIMM socket. (For a more detailed discussion of memory modules, see Part 5). However, because a large number of legacy systems still in place use 72-pin SIMM sockets, I have included those for reference as well.

SIMM Sockets

Two spring clips hold the SIMM module in place. In order to insert it, tilt the module about 15° forward, seat it into the slot and tilt the chip back until it snaps into place. SIMM modules were originally available in 30-pin, but that style has been obsolete for some time. About all you are likely to encounter are 72-pin SIMMs (**Figure 3.3**).

DIMM Sockets

DIMM modules (also in **Figure 3.3**) are also held in place by two clips, but the clips are not spring loaded. The chip is not tilted for installation, but rather seated straight down into the socket. Press firmly down on the top edge of the chip, applying equal force on both sides, until the clips snap in place around the module.

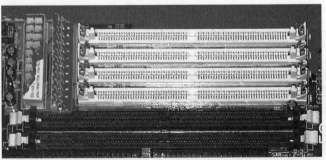

Figure 3.3 This illustration shows a pair of SIMM sockets side-by-side with a pair of DIMM sockets.

DIMM sockets are available in a wide variety of packages. These include the standard DIMMs used in desktops, SO-DIMMs used in laptops and other devices, and Micro-DIMMs seen in notebooks, sub-notebooks, and printers. One characteristic of SO-DIMMs and Micro-DIMMs that they share with SIMMs is that they are installed at an angle into spring clip sockets. **Table 3.6** lists these sockets and the memory typically associated to them.

For more information on The Packaging of Memory, go to page 183, Chapter 9 of *The Complete Guide to A+ Certification*.

DIMM Sockets and Associated Memory Types

Socket Type	Associated Memory
168-pin DIMM	EDO, SDRAM, ECC
184-pin DIMM	DDR and RAMBUS
240-pin DIMM	DDR-2
100-pin SO-DIMM	EDO and SDRAM
144-pin SO-DIMM	EDO, SDRAM and DDR
200-pin SO-DIMM	DDR, DDR-2
172-pin Micro-DIMM	DDR

Table 3.6: The types of memory associated with DIMM modules

Port Identification on ATX Motherboards

In 1999, Microsoft and Intel cooperated in creating a color-coding standard for all ports used on the back of ATX motherboards. Oddly enough this is called the PC-99 Color Codes. In this fashion, all users, regardless of experience, will be able to easily install all peripherals and plugs as long as they have good color vision. **Table 3.7** lists the ports and their color codes. The illustration on the cover of this book shows the color codes at work.

For more information on Form Factor, go to page 112, Chapter 6 of *The Complete Guide to A+ Certification*.

PC-99 ATX Color Coding

Color	Port	Type of Port
Blue	Analog VGA	15-pin D-sub
White	Digital VGA	29-pin keyed
Burgundy	Parallel port	25-pin D-sub
Turquoise	Serial port	9-pin D-sub
Light blue	Audio line in	1/8" audio
Light green	Audio line out	1/8" audio
Pink	Microphone	1/8" audio
Orange	Speaker out	1/8" audio
Brown	R to L speaker connector	1/8" audio
Gray	IEEE-1394	6-pin keyed
Gold	Midi/game port	15-pin D-sub
Green	Mouse	Mini-DIN
Purple	Keyboard	Mini-DIN
Black	USB	Slotted

Table 3.7: The plugs on the backs of most computers these days are color-coded.

Cable Connections

Three primary types of cables connect to the motherboard: power cables from the power supply, ribbon cables for disk drives (and possibly the front I/O panel), and leads to connect fans or peripheral devices. For the most part, these can't be plugged into the wrong slots.

Power Cables

Cables that connect the power supply to the motherboard are easily recognized. The main power coming off the power supply on all modern systems is a 20-pin cable (**Figure 3.4**) with a notched key and connectors designed to prevent plugging the cable in backwards.

Figure 3.4 The ATX power connector. Notice how some of the holes are polygonal and some are square. Now you know what they mean by putting a square peg in a round hole.

ATX12V and CFX12V are specifications that standardize the power supplies used with Pentium 4-based computers. The P4 CPU requires an extra 12V power connector (**Figure 3.5**) from the power supply. This is a small 4-conductor cable with a clip on the connector to assure proper alignment.

Figure 3.5 Power supplies compatible with Pentium 4 CPUs will always have a 12V, 4-conductor connector for powering the CPU.

Ribbon Cables

Ribbon cables are used to connect most drives in the system, including many types of SCSI drives, IDE drives, and floppy disk drives. On some models of computer, a ribbon cable interconnects the front panel to the system board. Ribbon cables vary quite a bit in the number of conductors, and they vary somewhat in the connector used. One thing they all have in common is that the conductors are numbered from 1 to the end. The number 1 conductor on the ribbon cable is always shaded, as shown in **Figure 3.6**.

Figure 3.6   The number 1 conductor on a ribbon cable is the one with the colored insulator.

Floppy Disk: 34-pin connector, usually keyed. On two-device cables, conductors 10 through 17 will be twisted around between the middle connector and the end (**Figure 3.7**). This assures that the device on the end will be the bootable device. The 34th conductor is the drive change indicator. If this conductor is broken or shorted, the OS will not know when the disk in the drive has been changed and will show the same directory on repeated reads.

For more information on The Floppy Cable, go to page 265, Chapter 12 of *The Complete Guide to A+ Certification.*

IDE Cables: 40- or 80-conductor ribbon cables with 40-pin connectors (even on the 80-pin cables). These hook up to hard disk drives, tape drives, and CD/DVD drives. IDE cables can be configured to be cable select (CS). If the drives attached to the cable are set for cable select, the position on the cable determines if the device is master or slave. 40-conductor devices are set to CS by clipping the 28th conductor. 80-conductor cables are always CS. On a 40-conductor CS cable, the middle device will be master, and on an 80-conductor CS cable, the end device is master. 80-conductor cable-select cables are color coded as shown in **Table 3.8**.

For more information on Installing a Hard Drive, go to page 330, Chapter 14 of *The Complete Guide to A+ Certification.*

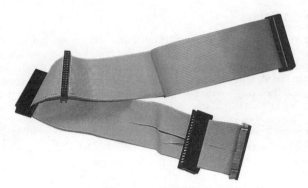

Figure 3.7 The floppy cable is the twisted one

Cable Select Color Coding

Color	Position	Role
Blue	End	Attaches to motherboard
Gray	Middle	Attaches to slave device
Black	End	Attaches to master device

Table 3.8: 80-conductor IDE cables are always cable select and are color coded to indicate what drive connects to which connector.

I/O Cable: Dell (and some other manufacturers as well) connect the front panel of the enclosure to the motherboard using a ribbon cable as well. This will be a 16-conductor ribbon that is keyed for proper installation.

Fan Leads

The wires that provide current to the cooling fans, either on the case or the CPU cooling fan, are 2-conductor wires with small black clips.

For more information on Temperature Control, go to page 95, Chapter 5 of *The Complete Guide to A+ Certification.*

Newer motherboards have three leads. The third lead controls fan speed relative to temperature.

BIOS Configuration

Before you can configure the BIOS, you need to be able to get into it. Different manufacturers have different key sequences that you must press to access the CMOS setup utility. Generally, the BIOS manufacturer provides the key sequence on the initial boot screen. However, sometimes motherboard or system manufacturers add a graphical overlay called a splash screen. Most of the time, you can get rid of the

For more information on BIOS, go to page 116, Chapter 6 of *The Complete Guide to A+ Certification.*

splash screen by pressing <Esc>. If this doesn't work, you're going to need help. **Table 3.9** is not all-inclusive, and there may be some exceptions to these

sequences, even within brands. But it should give you the right information the vast majority of the time.

Common Key Sequences for Entering BIOS Setup

BIOS Brand	Key Sequence
Acer	<Ctrl>+<Alt>+<Esc>
AMI	Delete OR F1 OR F2
Award	Delete OR <Ctrl>+<Alt>+<Esc>
Dell	F1
Gateway 2000	F1
Hewlett Packard	F1
Mr. BIOS	Esc OR <Ctrl>+<Alt>+<Esc> if Memory Test is completed
Phoenix	F1 OR F2 OR <Ctrl>+<Alt>+<Esc> OR <Ctrl>+<Alt>+<Insert>
Sony	Press and hold F3 while starting the computer

Table 3.9: Every version of BIOS has a key sequence for entering CMOS setup.

BIOS settings vary from manufacturer to manufacturer, but for the most part, they are very similar in what configuration changes they will allow you to make. Reporting each and every setting in the BIOS for every version written by every manufacturer would be a book in itself. What I've done in **Table 3.10** is to take a typical Award BIOS and break it down. Most manufacturers will have similar settings available, although they may vary in terms of how they are organized in the menus.

STANDARD AWARD CMOS SETUP

STANDARD FEATURES SETUP

Setting	Options	Description
Date	Page up/Page down	Changes system date
Time	Page up/Page down	Changes system time
Hard Disks/Type	Auto/User/None	Settings for IDE HDD
Hard Disks/Mode	Normal/LBA/Large/Auto	HDD translation method

continues

STANDARD FEATURES SETUP (*continued*)

Setting	Options	Description
Drive A	Various settings	Enables/disables Floppy A
Drive B	Various settings	Enables/disables Floppy B
Video	EGA/VGA, CGA-40, CGA-80, Mono	Establishes type of video used
Halt On	Various options	Stops POST on selected errors

BIOS FEATURES SETUP

Setting	Options	Description
Boot Virus Detection	Enabled/Disabled	Warns of any attempt to write to the boot sector
CPU Level 1 Cache	Enabled/Disabled	Enables read/write operations to L1 cache built into CPU
CPU Level 2 Cache	Enabled/Disabled	Enables read/write operations to L2 cache built into CPU
CPU Level 2 Cache ECC Check	Enabled/Disabled	Turns on/off ECC mode
Quick Power On Self Test	Enabled/Disabled	Full test/Tests only selected system components on cold boot
HDD Sequence	IDE/SCSI	Where to look for MBR
Boot Sequence	Options vary	Determines the order of devices in which POST looks for the MBR
Boot Up Floppy Seek	Enabled/Disabled	Tests floppy drive to see if it has forty or eighty tracks
Floppy Disk Access Control	R/W, Read Only	Security access for floppy drive
HDD Block Mode Sectors	Options vary	Instructs the hard disk controller to read and write in blocks of sectors rather than individual sectors. **Must** be turned off in WinNT
HDD S.M.A.R.T capability	Enabled/Disabled	Determines IDE SMART capable
PS2 Mouse Function Control	Enabled/Auto	Looks to PS2 for mouse
OS2 Onboard Memory	Enabled/Disabled	Use OS2 memory mapping
PCI/VGA Palette Snoop	Disabled/Enabled	Allows video adapters to directly access RAM looking for video information

Setting	Options	Description
Video ROM/BIOS Shadowing	Enabled/Disabled	Allows copying of BIOS routines to upper memory for enhanced performance
C8000-DFFFF Shadowing (multiple entries)	Enabled/Disabled	Allows copying of supplemental BIOS to specific addresses
Boot Up NumLock Status	On/Off	Determines whether number lock on keyboard is on or off after system boots
Typomatic Rate Setting	Disabled/Enabled	Disabled turns off Typomatic rate and Typomatic delay
Typomatic Rate	Options vary	Sets speed at which characters repeat when a key on the keyboard is held down
Typomatic Delay	Options vary	Sets time that elapses before keys begin to repeat when a key on the keyboard is held down
Security Option	System/Setup	Determines where security is controlled

CHIPSET FEATURES SETUP

Setting	Options	Description
EDO Autoconfiguration	Enabled/Disabled	Allows chipset to control EDO timing functions
EDO Read Burst Timing	Options vary	Sets number of clock cycles for Burst Mode read operations
EDO Write Burst Timing	Options vary	Sets number of clock cycles for Burst Mode write operations
EDO RAS Precharge	3T, 4T	Sets number of clock cycles for RAS
EDO RAS/CAS Delay	2T, 3T	Sets number of clock cycles for RAS/CAS delay
SDRAM Configuration	Varies	Sets clock speed of SDRAM
SDRAM RAS Precharge	Auto, 3T, 4T	Sets number of clock cycles for RAS
SDRAM RAS/CAS Delay	Auto, 3T, 2T	Sets number of clock cycles for RAS/CAS delay

continues

CHIPSET FEATURES SETUP (*continued*)

Setting	Options	Description
SDRAM Banks Close Policy	Arbitration, Page Miss	If set to Page Miss, all pages of data in the CPU cache will be flushed if the CPU goes idle
Graphics Aperture Size	Options vary	Sets the page size for the graphics card to use if it must use the system memory to augment its own
Video Memory Cache Mode	UC, USWC	Determines how video memory addresses cache
PCI 2.1 Support	Enabled/Disabled	Disabled setting drops system back to PCI Version 1.0
Memory Hole at 15M-16M	Enabled/Disabled	Enables/disables use of these memory addresses
Onboard FDC Controller	Enabled/Disabled	Allows you to disable the floppy disk drive
Onboard Floppy Swap A/B	Enabled/Disabled	Switches drives A and B
Onboard Serial Port 1	Various settings/Disabled	Allows reconfiguring or disabling Serial Port 1
Onboard Serial Port 2	Various settings/Disabled	Allows reconfiguring or disabling Serial Port 2
Onboard Parallel Port	Various settings/Disabled	Allows reconfiguring or disabling parallel port
Parallel Port Mode	Normal, ECC, ECC/ECP	Sets up parallel communications
ECP DMA Select	Options vary	Sets DMA channel used by ECP parallel mode
UART2 Use Infrared	Enabled/Disabled	Sets infrared port to UART2
Onboard PCI/IDE Enable	Both, Primary, Secondary, Disabled	Enables/disables IDE ports
IDE DMA Mode	Auto/Disable	Disables, autoselects Direct Memory Access
IDE 0/1 – Master/Slave	Options vary	Sets PIO mode and DMA channel for specific device

POWER MANAGEMENT SETUP

Setting	Options	Description
Power Management	User Defined, Disabled, Min, Max	Determines PM method
Video Off Option	Suspend→Off, Always On	Determines how the monitor is managed

Setting	Options	Description
Video Off Method	Options vary	Determines method by which monitor is shut down
HDD Power Down	Options vary	How long before hard drive shuts down
Suspend Mode	Options vary	How long before hard drive goes into suspended mode
PWR Button	Soft-off, Suspend, No Function	Determines how the power button affects power supply
Power Up on Modem ACT	Enabled/Disabled	Determines if modem wakes machine
AC Power Loss Restart	Enabled/Disabled	Automatically restarts machine when AC power is restored
Wake on LAN	Enabled/Disabled	Determines if NIC wakes machine

PNP AND PCI SETUP

Setting	Options	Description
PNP OS Installed?	Yes/No	Is the operating system PnP compliant?
Slot 1-? IRQ (several entries)	Auto, various settings	Manually assign an IRQ to a specific slot or let PnP handle allocations?
PCI Latency Timer	Options vary	Number of clock cycles for PCI latency
IRQ 3-15 Used by ISA (several entries)	Yes/No	Is this IRQ assigned to a legacy ISA device?
Force Update ESCD	Enabled/Disabled	Forces reallocation of resources on POST
LOAD BIOS DEFAULTS?	Reloads factory settings. No internal settings.	
SUPERVISOR PASSWORD	Allows entry of supervisor password	
USER PASSWORD	Allows entry of user password	
IDE HDD AUTODETECT	Automatically detects and configures devices on Primary and Secondary IDE ports	

Table 3.10: Between the various brands of BIOS, there are far more different settings than the ones listed here, and the wording isn't always the same. However, this should give you a good head start in figuring out your BIOS settings.

Fine-Tuning BIOS Configuration

Most manufacturers are very conservative on the factory default settings they provide. They prefer to err on the side of caution rather than
performance. In the following paragraphs, I'm going to make some
suggestions that might boost the performance of your PC noticeably.
Or it might lock it up like a stone. So before you start poking around,
use a CMOS backup utility or make sure you have a recent flash BIOS
burned to a bootable floppy just in case.

SDRAM TIMING or CAS Latency: This refers to how many clock
cycles elapse from a Row Access cycle to a column access cycle. These
are clock cycles where the memory is simply lying dormant. With
SDRAM, this will be set to either 2 or 3 clock cycles. The factory default
is frequently set to 3. The idea is that slower is safer. RAM doesn't mind
waiting an extra clock cycle. But if it jumps to CAS too soon, your system
will lock up. Memory is rated as CAS Latency 2 (CL2) or CL3. If you
are running CL2 memory on a system configured to CL3, you are
wasting one third of your clock cycles during a typical memory read.

AGP Capability: Many motherboards are capable of supporting AGP
cards up to 8x. Typically, Plug 'n Play detects the video card all right, so
everything seems fine and good. What doesn't get automatically configured on many system boards is the AGP mode. By default, many
motherboards ship with the factory defaults set to AGP 2x. Aren't you
glad to discover that your brand new AGP 8x video card has been poking along at 2x all this time?

CPU Cache ECC Check: On a typical system using modern memory,
memory errors occur about once in every two or three trillion clock
cycles. Contrary to popular opinion, not all memory errors are fatal.
Your system ignores the vast majority of them. If your BIOS allows disabling ECC checking, this eliminates the process of calculating the error
correction code. It can result in a boost of system performance of up to
2 percent. The down side is that if you're running a server, you don't
want any error messages. Use this trick only on gaming machines.

Onboard Device Configuration: Disable all onboard devices that are
not being used. If you have onboard sound but no speakers, disable the
sound chip. If you have an onboard NIC or modem but don't use them,
take them out. This doesn't speed up overall system performance, but it
does speed up the boot process. In addition, with most motherboards,
this procedure will force the system to relinquish the resources that
were being used by those devices so that you can use those resources
on devices that you do need. This is particularly true of system boards
with onboard SCSI. SCSI chips will always load their BIOS during
POST even if there are no devices attached, unless they are disabled.

Spread Spectrum Modulation (or Control): This feature was added
to high-speed system boards as a way to reduce the amount of EMI a

board emits. By doing so, the feature is actually reducing the overall performance of your system by up to 5 percent. If you are in an area where EMI from your system will not affect others or won't screw up your spouse's TV reception, turn this off. The down side to turning it off is that it has the overall effect of boosting your system bus speed by as much as 10 percent. If your memory or CPU is already performing nominally at its maximum speed, this can cause your system to either refuse to boot, or to crash sporadically.

AGP Fast Write: AGP Fast Write is the capability many chipsets possess of allowing the AGP card to accelerate data transfers from system memory to the video card. Yet by factory default, this feature is not enabled. (Note that transfers from the video card to memory are not affected.) Read operations from memory can be increased by as much as 10 percent if this option is enabled. One possible side effect is that PCI devices might start to behave erratically. Give it a try, and if your NIC stops working, go back to square one.

System Bus Speed: This option is not available on all chipsets. However, there are a few that allow you to gradually increase the speed of the front side bus in increments of as little as 1MHz. Since CPU clock speeds are now locked into the bus speed, this is the one way you have of overclocking the CPU. Be careful with this setting, though. You're also forcing your memory to run faster as well. Overclocking memory can result in data error or intermittent system lockups if the installed memory moduals aren't up to the task. Bumping the bus speed also makes your CPU, your chipset, and your RAM run hotter. So if you're going to play this game, make sure your cooling system is up to the task.

CPU Core Voltage: This is another setting that you won't find in all CMOS setup routines. It is a setting that goes hand in hand with overclocking. When you make your CPU run faster, sometimes you need to boost the core voltage in order to make it keep pace. If you are getting intermittent lockups after boosting your front side bus speed, try making minor adjustments with this setting. Increasing the core voltage will only exacerbate the effect of overclocking in terms of how hot your CPU runs, though. This can be a dangerous game to play.

BIOS and Security

When setting security on systems, the BIOS is the first place you should start. There are a few features in most brands of BIOS that allow you to do some to increase security:

- ✔ BIOS setup passwords
- ✔ System access passwords
- ✔ Device activation
- ✔ Keyboard lockdown

Passwords

With most versions of BIOS, you can set two different passwords on a system. You can configure the system to require a user to type in a password in order to boot the system, and you can configure a totally different password for someone to get in and play around with CMOS settings. BIOS manufacturers vary in terms of how long this password can be. Most allow a maximum of 13 characters; some as few as 8.

So what happens if a user sets a password on a system just before walking out in a huff? All is not lost. Many motherboard manufacturers have a jumper on the board that will allow you to reset the CMOS settings to factory defaults, and factory defaults include no configured passwords.

If your system has no jumper for this purpose, removing the clock battery from the motherboard, counting to a hundred, and then replacing it can accomplish the same thing. This forces the capacitors that provide current to the CMOS chip while the battery is being changed to discharge completely before you reinstall the battery.

Okay, you've looked all over the motherboard and there is no jumper. Removing the battery and counting to a thousand didn't do the trick. Now what? Many BIOS manufacturers over the years have provided "back door" passwords into the CMOS setup just in case this happened. Most of these back doors are undocumented and have really been discovered by trial and error, and by technicians like me wheedling the tech support people into confessing. Below, I've listed a few back doors people have found over the years. Not every back door password works with every version of the BIOS with which it is listed, so a little trial and error might be in order. Remember that these passwords are all case-sensitive, so make sure your CAPS lock and NUM lock are set right.

AMI BIOS Back Door Passwords

AMI	HEWITT RAND	A.M.I.
AAAMMMIII	AMI?SW	CONDO
BIOS	AMI_SW	
PASSWORD	LKWPETER	

PHOENIX BIOS Back Door Passwords

phoenix	CMOS	BIOS
PHOENIX		

AWARD BIOS Back Door Passwords

ALFAROME	CONDO	SER
ALLy	Condo	SKY_FOX
aLLy	d8on	SYXZ
aLLY	djonet	syxz
ALLY	HLT	shift + syxz
aPAf	J64	TTPTHA
_award	J256	ZAAADA
AWARD_SW	J262	ZBAAACA
AWARD?SW	j332	ZJAAADC
AWARD SW	j322	01322222
AWARD PW	KDD	589589
AWKWARDø	Lkwpeter	589721
awkward	LKWPETER	595595
BIOSTAR	PINT	598598
CONCAT	pint	

Other Manufacturers' Backdoor Passwords

Manufacturer	Password
Biostar	Biostar
Compaq	Compaq
Dell	Dell
Enox	xo11nE
Epox	central
Freetech	Posterie
IWill	iwill
Jetway	spooml
Packard Bell	bell9
QDI	QDI
Siemens	SKY_FOX
TMC	BIGO
Toshiba	Toshiba
VOBIS & IBM	merlin

Table 3.11: Most BIOS manufacturers provide a back door password for getting into the CMOS setup in case the owner gets locked out.

Device Activation

Another step you can take in securing systems is to inactivate devices that are either not necessary or are potential information leaks. For example, anyone can bring a floppy diskette into his or her office, copy data, and take it home. Also USB Flash memory devices (as of this writing) are available up to 4GB. That's a lot of data that can be stored on a device easily concealed anywhere on the body. If security is an issue, shut it down.

In the Integrated Peripherals section of the CMOS, floppy drives can be set to a number of different sizes and capacities, including certain drives that haven't been manufactured for years. (All I want for Christmas is a 5.25" 360K floppy disk drive!) Another setting is to totally disable the floppy drives. Doing so will close that hole. If a machine is going to sit inactive for any amount of time, the same thing can be done to IDE Channel 0 and IDE Channel 1.

Disabling USB ports is also possible as long as you don't have any devices that require USB. Unfortunately USB is either all or none. If you have to enable USB for one device, that makes the empty USB ports available for the USB flash memory devices. Fortunately, most operating systems have methods of disabling removable storage devices.

Keyboard Lockdown

Using this feature requires that both your motherboard and system enclosure support it. If they do, a system whose enclosure features a keylock that links to the motherboard via a small cable can be secured in this manner. When Security in the CMOS is set to look for the lock, if a user tries to type anything when the system case is in the locked position, he or she will get one of the various A20 error messages listed later this chapter, and the system won't boot.

Flashing BIOS

Most modern BIOS chips are flash BIOS. By this, I mean that, should you need to update the code stored on the chip, a piece of software will do that for you. When a new BIOS is available from a motherboard or system manufacturer, it will typically post that new version on the support pages of its Web site. A key rule of thumb about BIOS upgrades is,

For more information on The Address Bus and BIOS, go to page 116, Chapter 6 of *The Complete Guide to A+ Certification.*

"If it ain't broke, don't fix it!" If there is a good reason for changing your BIOS, go ahead and do it. Good reasons would include a new type of device that is now available that your old BIOS version doesn't support, or the fact that the manufacturer detected a serious bug in the previous version. A bad reason for upgrading is, "It's new, so it's gotta be better!"

If you and your manufacturer have agreed that upgrading your BIOS is the ideal way to solve a specific problem you are having, you can save yourself a few headaches by following some simple procedures.

1. Back up your system! A failed BIOS upgrade can leave your system dead in the water. It's extremely rare to kill a system by performing a BIOS upgrade, but it has been known to happen. Always prepare for the worst, and thank your lucky stars when that preparation was a waste of time.
2. Write down any custom configurations you may have set.
3. Use a CMOS recovery utility to back up your existing BIOS configuration. You might need that later on, too.
4. Download the files you will need for the upgrade. Usually, this consists of the flash utility that will be used to perform the upgrade and the data file that contains the new BIOS code.
5. Scan these files for viruses. Hackers find their way into everything, including manufacturers' FTP servers.
6. Create a bootable floppy diskette and copy the two scanned files to that floppy. Write down the name of the flash utility.
7. Boot your machine to the floppy diskette, and once you have an A prompt, type in the command for the flash utility. It will ask you what version of BIOS you want to use for the upgrade and display all of the available options. In your case, it is most likely all of those options. While the new code is being burned to the BIOS chip, **do not power off your system for any reason**. This will kill your system.
8. Once the flash utility tells you the process is completed, remove the floppy from the drive and reboot the machine.
9. If you require configurations outside the factory default, press the appropriate key sequence to enter the CMOS setup utility and make your changes. If all went well, you're good to go.

Recovering from a Failed BIOS Upgrade

It didn't go so well, huh? Bummer! Oh well, perhaps all is not lost. There is something manufacturers often do to help recover from a failed BIOS upgrade. This is called BOOTBLOCK. If your system is equipped with BOOTBLOCK, it possesses a secondary BIOS chip with just enough information to boot your machine to the floppy disk. Using another machine, you can get a fresh copy of the BIOS, or if the new version was what killed you, you can use a copy of the older version to reflash your BIOS.

With some of these boards, simply the fact that the primary BIOS chip can't be read is sufficient to induce the machine to invoke BOOT-BLOCK. Another method used by some manufacturers is to include a Flash Recovery jumper on the motherboard. If the system doesn't automatically invoke BOOTBLOCK after a failed upgrade, and you know the system is equipped with BOOTBLOCK, check and see if this jumper exists. You may have to move the jumper to Recovery Mode in order to bypass the primary BIOS chip.

As a last resort, if your BIOS chip is a DIPP module, you might be able to order a new chip from the manufacturer. That's where the IC puller in your toolkit comes in handy.

Diagnosing Beep Codes

Different manufacturers have different signals they send out through the PC speaker when the system can't boot as far as the video display. Unfortunately, there is no uniform standard for beep codes. The following tables list some of the more popular manufacturers' codes. Remember, however, that there is a lot of variance between different versions even by the same manufacturer.

AMI BIOS Beep Codes

Beep Sequence	Cause of Error	Possible Solution
1 short	DRAM refresh failure	Failure of the programmable interrupt or possibly the interrupt controller. Problem with the motherboard.
2 short	Memory parity error	Parity read error in the lower 64K. Bad chip.
3 short	Base 64K memory failure	Memory read/write error in the lower 64K of RAM. Bad chip.
4 short	System timer failure	Usually means that the system clock/timer failed. That's a problem with the motherboard. It can also indicate there is a memory error in the first bank of memory. Try swapping out memory before replacing the board.
5 short	Processor initialization error	System got power. CPU didn't run POST.
6 short	Gate A20 error	This is a problem with the keyboard. If replacing the keyboard doesn't help, it's the KB controller on the motherboard.
7 short	Virtual mode processor exception error	Bad CPU just about every time.
8 short	Read/write error in the video card memory	Try reseating the video card. If this doesn't work try a new card.

Beep Sequence	Cause of Error	Possible Solution
9 short	ROM checksum error	The system BIOS ROM is probably corrupted and needs to be replaced. If it's a flashable BIOS, flash a new one. If not, order a new ROM-BIOS chip.
10 short	CMOS shutdown register read/write error	The shutdown for the CMOS has failed
11 short	Cache error	Bad L2 cache. If the L2 is in the CPU, that means replacing the CPU.
1 long, 2 short	Video card failure	Try reseating the video card. If this doesn't work try a new card.
1 long, 3 short	Memory test failure	POST detected bad system RAM. Try replacing the memory modules.
1 long, 8 short	Display test failure	Try reseating the video card. If this doesn't work try a new card.
2 short	POST failure	One of the hardware tests failed, but the BIOS doesn't have a clue which one.
1 long	POST has passed all tests	This is the one beep you **want** to hear.

Table 3.12

Award BIOS Beep Codes

Beep Sequence	Cause of Error	Possible Solution
1 long, 2 short	Video adapter error	Make sure the video card is seated properly. If it is and the problem won't go away, try a different card.
Constant beeps	Memory fault	Make sure memory is installed. Make sure all modules are properly seated. If neither is the case, try new memory.
1 long, 3 short	Video memory not detected	Make sure the video card is properly seated. If this doesn't help, try a different card.
High frequency beeps while system is running	CPU is running hot	Make sure the CPU fan is working properly. Make sure that nothing is blocking the ventilation holes in the enclosure.
Repeating high/low	CPU error	CPU may not be seated properly. CPU may have failed, or it may be overheated. See above.

Table 3.13

Compaq BIOS Beep Codes

Beep Sequence	Cause of Error	Possible Solution
1 short	No error	Get to work.
1 long, 1 short	BIOS ROM checksum error	If possible, reload the BIOS from the Restore CD.
2 short	General error	Occurs because of so many things it's useless.
1 long, 2 short	Video error	Make sure the video card is properly seated. If this doesn't help, try a different card.
7 beeps— 4 alternating long and short followed by 1 long and 2 short	AGP video	Make sure the video card is properly seated. If this doesn't help, try a different card. This code is specific to Compaq Deskpro systems.
1 long neverending beep	Bad RAM	Check to make sure memory is properly seated. If so, replace memory module.
1 short, 2 long	Bad RAM	Check to make sure memory is properly seated. If so, replace memory module.

Table 3.14

Dell BIOS Beep Codes

Beep Sequence*	Cause of Error	Possible Solution
1 – 2	Video card not detected	Try reseating the video card. If error recurs, consider replacing card.
1 - 2 - 2 – 3	BIOS ROM checksum error	If possible, reset CMOS to factory defaults. If this doesn't work, flash a new version of the BIOS.
1 - 3 - 1 – 1	DRAM refresh error	Make sure memory modules are firmly seated. Run diagnostics on memory. If memory fails diagnostics, replace it.
1 - 3 - 1 – 3	Keyboard Controller error	Make sure keyboard is plugged in firmly. If this does not solve problem, try a new keyboard.
1 - 3 - 3 – 1	Memory not present or failed to pass diagnostics	Make sure memory modules are firmly seated. Run diagnostics on memory. If memory fails diagnostics, replace it.

Beep Sequence*	Cause of Error	Possible Solution
1 - 3 - 4 – 1	Memory failed diagnostics.	Make sure memory modules are firmly seated. Run diagnostics on memory. If memory fails diagnostics, replace it.
1 - 3 - 4 – 3	Failure in lower memory registers	Make sure memory modules are firmly seated. Run diagnostics on memory. If memory fails diagnostics, replace it.
1 - 4 - 1 - 1	Failure in higher memory registers	Make sure memory modules are firmly seated. Run diagnostics on memory. If memory fails diagnostics, replace it.

* Beep codes are represented as BEEP pause BEEP pause BEEP. In other words, 4-2-3 would be interpreted as four beeps, a noticeable pause, two more beeps, a noticeable pause, and finally three beeps.

Table 3.15

IBM Desktop BIOS Beep Codes

Beep Sequence	Cause of Error	Possible Solution
1 short	No error	Stop trying to diagnose the problem.
2 short	Initialization error	The error code displayed on the screen indicates the problem.
1 long, 1 short	System board failure	Replace motherboard.
1 long, 2 short	Video adapter error	If using a separate adapter, make sure video card is seated. If this isn't the problem, replace video card. If onboard video, replace motherboard.
1 long, 3 short	EGA/VGA adapter error	If using a separate adapter, make sure video card is seated. If this isn't the problem, replace video card. If onboard video, replace motherboard.
3 long	3270 keyboard adapter error	Replace keyboard.
Continuous	Power supply error	Replace the power supply.
9 long, 9 short	Power supply error	Replace the power supply.
No beep	Power supply absent	Replace the power supply.

Table 3.16

IBM Thinkpad BIOS Beep Codes

Beep Sequence	Cause of Error	Possible Solution
Continuous beeping	System board failure	Replace motherboard.
1 short	Video adapter or LCD failure; possibly power supply or system board as well	Try reseating all cables between system board and LCD. Test power supply voltages.
1 short (May receive message "Unable to access boot source")	Most likely hard disk failure; may be system board failure	May simply mean the disk hasn't been initialized. If the disk was working before, see if the CMOS detects it. If not, possible bad drive. If a new hard disk is available, try replacing the drive. If this fails, it's the motherboard.
1 long, 2 short	System board, video adapter, or LCD assembly	In order: Probable system board failure. If under warranty, have a video adapter sent as well. If these don't fix it, it's the LCD.
1 long, 4 short	Low battery voltage	Charge battery. If it won't hold a charge, replace it.
1 short every second	Low battery voltage	Charge battery. If it won't hold a charge, replace it.
2 short with error codes	POST failure	This error doesn't provide enough information to be useful.
2 short	System board failure	Replace system board.

Table 3.17

Mylex BIOS Beep Codes

Beep Sequence	Cause of Error	Possible Solution
1 short	Normal boot	Why are you troubleshooting?
2 short	Video adapter error	The video adapter is either faulty or not seated properly. Check the adapter.
3 short	Keyboard controller error	Replace the keyboard.
4 short	Keyboard error	Replace the keyboard. If this doesn't help, the keyboard controller on the motherboard is faulty.

Beep Sequence	Cause of Error	Possible Solution
5 short	PIC 0 error	Programmable Interrupt Controller failed. Bad motherboard.
6 short	PIC 1 error	Programmable Interrupt Controller failed. Bad motherboard.
7 short	DMA page register error	May be the DMA controller, may be caused by device. Remove sound cards and floppy cable and reboot. If problem persists, replace motherboard.
8 short	RAM refresh error	May be bad memory, may be a bad memory control circuit. Try replacing the RAM modules one by one. If this doesn't help, replace motherboard.
9 short	RAM data error	May be bad memory, may be a bad memory control circuit. Try replacing the RAM modules one by one. If this doesn't help, replace motherboard.
10 short	RAM parity error	May be bad memory, may be a bad memory control circuit. Try replacing the RAM modules one by one. If this doesn't help, replace motherboard.
11 short	DMA controller 0 error	May be the DMA controller, may be caused by device. Remove sound cards and floppy cable and reboot. If problem persists, replace motherboard.
12 short	CMOS RAM error	This isn't the system memory. Replace motherboard.
13 short	DMA controller 1 error	May be the DMA controller, may be caused by device. Remove sound cards and floppy cable and reboot. If problem persists, replace motherboard.
14 short	CMOS RAM battery error	Replace battery on motherboard.
15 short	CMOS RAM checksum error	This isn't the system memory. Replace motherboard.
16 short	BIOS ROM checksum error	If possible, flash a new BIOS. If not flash BIOS, replace BIOS chip.

Table 3.18

Phoenix BIOS Beep Codes

Beep Sequence*	Cause of Error	Possible Solution
1-1-2	CPU test failure	Bad CPU. Replace it.
Low 1-1-2	System board select failure	Undetermined problem with motherboard. Disconnect all cables and remove RAM. If the problem persists, replace motherboard. If not, troubleshoot new beep codes.
1-1-3	CMOS read/write error	If possible, flash a new BIOS. If not flash BIOS, replace BIOS chip.
Low 1-1-3	Extended CMOS RAM failure	CMOS RAM above 1MB has failed. Replace the CMOS chip if possible.
1-1-4	BIOS ROM checksum error	If possible, flash a new BIOS. If not flash BIOS, replace BIOS chip.
1-2-1	PIT failure	Programmable Interrupt Timer failed. Replace motherboard.
1-2-2	DMA failure	May be the DMA controller, may be caused by device. Remove sound cards and floppy cable and reboot. If problem persists, replace motherboard.
1-2-3	DMA read/write failure	May be the DMA controller, may be caused by device. Remove sound cards and floppy cable and reboot. If problem persists, replace motherboard.
1-3-1	RAM refresh failure	Memory control circuitry has failed. Replace motherboard.
1-3-2	64KB RAM failure	Replace memory module in first bank.
1-3-3	First 64KB RAM failure	Replace memory module in first bank.
1-3-4	First 64KB logic failure	Replace memory module in first bank.
1-4-1	Address line failure	May be a memory problem, may be a problem with the motherboard. Replace memory module in first bank. If this doesn't help, replace motherboard.
1-4-2	Parity RAM failure	Replace memory module in first bank.
1-4-3	EISA fail-safe timer test	Replace the motherboard.
1-4-4	EISA NMI port 462 test	Replace the motherboard.

Beep Sequence*	Cause of Error	Possible Solution
2-1-1	64KB RAM failure	Replace memory module in first bank.
2-1-2	64KB RAM failure	Replace memory module in first bank.
2-1-3	64KB RAM failure	Replace memory module in first bank.
2-1-4	64KB RAM failure	Replace memory module in first bank.
2-2-1	64KB RAM failure	Replace memory module in first bank.
2-2-2	64KB RAM failure	Replace memory module in first bank.
2-2-3	64KB RAM failure	Replace memory module in first bank.
2-2-4	64KB RAM failure	Replace memory module in first bank.
2-3-1	64KB RAM failure	Replace memory module in first bank.
2-3-2	64KB RAM failure	Replace memory module in first bank.
2-3-3	64KB RAM failure	Replace memory module in first bank.
2-3-4	64KB RAM failure	Replace memory module in first bank.
2-4-1	64KB RAM failure	Replace memory module in first bank.
2-4-2	64KB RAM failure	Replace memory module in first bank.
2-4-3	64KB RAM failure	Replace memory module in first bank.
2-4-4	64KB RAM failure	Replace memory module in first bank.
3-1-1	Slave DMA register failure	May be the DMA controller, may be caused by device. Remove sound cards and floppy cable and reboot. If problem persists, replace motherboard.
3-1-2	Master DMA register failure	May be the DMA controller, may be caused by device. Remove sound cards and floppy cable and reboot. If problem persists, replace motherboard.
3-1-3	Master interrupt mask register failure	Replace the motherboard.

continues

Phoenix BIOS Beep Codes (*continued*)

Beep Sequence*	Cause of Error	Possible Solution
3-1-4	Slave interrupt mask register failure	Replace the motherboard.
3-2-2	Interrupt vector error	Replace the motherboard.
3-2-3	Reserved	Doesn't mean anything to you.
3-2-4	Keyboard controller failure	Try replacing keyboard. If that doesn't help, it's the controller on the motherboard.
3-3-1	CMOS RAM power bad	Replace the CMOS battery.
3-3-2	CMOS configuration error	Replace CMOS battery and restore settings.
3-3-3	Reserved	Doesn't mean anything to you.
3-3-4	Video memory failure	Make sure the video card is properly seated. If this doesn't help, try a different card. This code is specific to Compaq Deskpro systems.
3-4-1	Video initialization failure	Make sure the video card is properly seated. If this doesn't help, try a different card. This code is specific to Compaq Deskpro systems.
4-2-1	Timer failure	Replace motherboard.
4-2-2	Shutdown failure	Replace motherboard.
4-2-3	Gate A20 failure	Try replacing keyboard. If that fails, it's the controller on the motherboard.
4-2-4	Unexpected interrupt in protected mode	CPU failure. Replace CPU.
4-3-1	RAM test failure	Replace the motherboard.
4-3-3	Interval timer channel 2 failure	Replace the motherboard.
4-3-4	Time of day clock failure	Replace the motherboard.
4-4-1	Serial port failure	Replace the motherboard.
4-4-2	Parallel port failure	Replace the motherboard.
4-4-3	Math coprocessor failure	Replace CPU.

* Beep codes are represented as BEEP pause BEEP pause BEEP. In other words, 4-2-3 would be interpreted as four beeps, a noticeable pause, two more beeps, a noticeable pause, and finally three beeps.

Table 3.19

Text Error Messages at Startup

If a system gets far enough into POST that video is initialized, many BIOS manufacturers have their own ubiquitous little messages they flash on the screen in the event of an error. Not all of them are self explanatory and some are downright arcane. As best as I could, I have accumulated messages from different BIOS manufacturers defining their text error messages. If you are getting numbers, relax. I'll get to that later on.

AMI Text Messages

Error Message	Cause of Error	Possible Solution
A20 error	Keyboard failure	Problem with the keyboard controller. Replace keyboard and try again.
Address line short	Probable system board failure	Replace system board.
Bad PnP serial ID checksum	PCI device responded with invalid device ID	Try reseating the device in the slot and restarting. If this doesn't resolve the issue, replace the device.
CMOS battery state low	Bad battery	Replace the battery on the motherboard.
CMOS checksum invalid	CMOS configuration is invalid	CMOS configuration is invalid. Check the battery, restore to factory defaults and try again.
CMOS display type mismatch	Invalid display configuration in CMOS	Display settings in CMOS do not match the type detected by the BIOS. Run setup.
CMOS memory size mismatch	POST reported an error in RAM	The amount of memory detected by POST is different from the amount indicated in CMOS. Run setup.
CMOS time and date not set	Self-explanatory	You might want to try setting the time and date.
Diskette boot failure	System could not boot to diskette	The diskette in Drive A is not bootable or is corrupt. Get another diskette.
DMA #1 error	DMA Controller responded with error	May be the DMA controller, may be caused by device. Remove sound cards and floppy cable and reboot. If problem persists, replace motherboard.

continues

AMI Text Messages (*continued*)

Error Message	Cause of Error	Possible Solution
DMA #2 error	DMA Controller responded with error	May be the DMA controller, may be caused by device. Remove sound cards and floppy cable and reboot. If problem persists, replace motherboard.
DMA bus timeout	DMA Controller responded with error	A device has tied up a DMA channel for more than 7.8 microseconds. If the problem is persistent, you may have a bad chipset. Replace the motherboard.
DMA error	DMA Controller responded with error	May be the DMA controller, may be caused by device. Remove sound cards and floppy cable and reboot. If problem persists, replace motherboard.
FDD controller failure	POST could not get a response from the floppy disk drive	Floppy drive could not be initialized. Check cables and try again. If no floppy is installed, set the CMOS accordingly.
Floppy disk controller resource conflict	IRQ, DMA, or I/O conflict with floppy drive	Make sure you didn't install a sound card and steal the floppy disk's DMA channel.
HDD controller failure	POST could not get a response from the hard disk drive	Hard drive could not be initialized. Check cables and try again. If no floppy is installed, set the CMOS accordingly.
I/O card parity error at xxxxx*	Memory residing on an expansion card responded with error	An expansion device with installed memory is returning a parity error. Replace device.
Insert bootable media	No boot device found	Check boot sequence in CMOS and try again.
INTR #1 error	Interrupt controller failure	Replace the motherboard.
INTR #2 error	Interrupt controller failure	Replace the motherboard.
Invalid boot diskette	System is attempting to boot to floppy and not finding MBR	The diskette in Drive A is not bootable or is corrupt. Get another diskette.
KB/Interface error	No keyboard detected	There is an error in the keyboard connector. First make sure the keyboard cable is properly seated. Next, try a known-good keyboard. If this fails, replace the motherboard.

Error Message	Cause of Error	Possible Solution
Keyboard error	Keyboard timing issue	There is a timing problem with the keyboard. Make sure the keyboard is connected. If that's not the problem, replace the keyboard.
Keyboard stuck key detected	The cat is on the keyboard	A stuck keyboard key was detected; move the cat.
Memory parity error at xxxxx*	System RAM is returning a parity error	Replace memory modules.
NVRAM CHECKSUM ERROR - NVRAM CLEARED	Contents of CMOS are being reported invalid	Reset CMOS to factory defaults and reboot. If this doesn't work, remove the motherboard battery for about sixty seconds, reinstall, and reboot. If this fails, replace the motherboard.
NVRAM cleared by jumper	The Clear CMOS jumper has been moved to the Clear position	Information in CMOS has been set to factory defaults. If there were any custom configurations they need to be restored.
NVRAM data invalid - NVRAM cleared	User settings in CMOS deleted	Reset CMOS to factory defaults and reboot. If this doesn't work, remove the motherboard battery for about sixty seconds, reinstall, and reboot. If this fails, replace the motherboard.
Off board parity error	Parity error detected on an expansion device	An expansion device with installed memory is returning a parity error. Replace device.
On board parity error	Parity error detected in system memory	System RAM is returning a parity error. Replace memory modules.
Parallel port resource conflict	I/O address or IRQ for parallel port is not available	Usually occurs with a secondary parallel port in an expansion card. Another device has taken IRQ 5. Check your sound card and see if it's on IRQ5. That's the usual culprit.
Parity error	System RAM is returning a parity error	Replace memory modules.
PCI error log is full	The PCI Error Log only holds 15 entries	You have surpassed this amount and no more entries will be logged. Try forcing a reset of all PnP devices.

continues

AMI Text Messages (*continued*)

Error Message	Cause of Error	Possible Solution
PCI I/O port conflict	I/O address conflict	If one device is manually configured, reset its configuration. If both devices are PnP, exchange slot positions on the motherboard.
PCI IRQ conflict	IRQ address conflict	If one device is manually configured, reset its configuration. If both devices are PnP, exchange slot positions on the motherboard.
PCI memory conflict	Memory address conflict	If one device is manually configured, reset its configuration. If both devices are PnP, exchange slot positions on the motherboard.
Primary boot device not found	Bootstrap loader does not point to a valid MBR	May simply mean the disk hasn't been initialized. If the disk was working before, see if the CMOS detects it. If not, possible bad drive. If a new hard disk is available, try replacing the drive. If this doesn't help, it's the motherboard.
Primary IDE controller resource conflict	I/O address or IRQ for primary IDE port is not available	The primary IDE controller has requested a resource that is already in use. This may happen on boards with additional IDE controller cards installed. Reconfigure the controller card to use different IRQs. Onboard ports are pretty picky about getting what they want.
Primary input device not found	Keyboard error	Usually means the keyboard wasn't found.
Run setup	Can mean anything	CMOS configuration is invalid. Check the battery, restore to factory defaults, and try again.
Secondary IDE controller resource conflict	I/O address or IRQ for secondary IDE port is not available	The secondary IDE controller has requested a resource that is already in use. This may happen on boards with additional IDE controller cards installed.
Serial port 1 resource conflict	I/O address or IRQ for primary serial port is not available	Serial port 1 has requested a resource that is already in use. Probably means that the IRQ has been reserved.

Error Message	Cause of Error	Possible Solution
Serial port 2 resource conflict	I/O address or IRQ for secondary serial port is not available	Serial port 2 has requested a resource that is already in use. Probably means that the IRQ has been reserved.
Static device resource conflict	I/O address or IRQ not available for statically configured device	A card that is not Plug 'n Play ISA has requested a resource that is already in use. Try reserving the IRQ in PnP PCI configuration.
System board device resource conflict	I/O address or IRQ for an undefined expansion device is not available	A card that is not Plug 'n Play ISA has requested a resource that is already in use. Try reserving the IRQ in PnP PCI configuration.
System halted	Nonmaskable interrupt	An error the CPU couldn't handle has brought the system to a stop. Not a darned thing you can do about this one. If the problem is persistent, run a full systems diagnostics. Any one of a thousand things can be causing it.
Timer channel 2 error	System timer failed	Replace motherboard.
Uncorrectable ECC error	Memory failure	ECC has returned more than one faulty bit in a packet. System halted. If the problem is persistent, run a stress test on the memory and see if you find a bad memory module.
Undetermined NMI	Nonmaskable interrupt	A nonmaskable interrupt which the CPU couldn't handle has occurred. See the previous notes on NMIs.

* xxxxx represents the hexadecimal alliteration of a memory address.

Table 3.20

AWARD Text Messages

Error Message	Cause of Error	Possible Solution
BIOS ROM checksum error - System halted	CMOS unreadable	If possible, flash a new BIOS. If not flash BIOS, replace BIOS chip.
CMOS battery failed	Dead battery	Replace the battery.
CMOS checksum error - Defaults loaded	CMOS unreadable	Check the battery and reconfigure BIOS setup.

continues

AWARD Text Messages (*continued*)

Error Message	Cause of Error	Possible Solution
CMOS checksum error disk boot failure, insert system disk and press Enter	CMOS unreadable	Check the battery and reconfigure BIOS setup.
CPU at nnn	CPU clock speed	Not an error. Displays the clock speed of the CPU.
Diskette drives or types mismatch error - Run setup	Floppy drive in configuration doesn't match installed floppy	Check CMOS settings and reboot.
Error encountered initializing hard drive	Hard drive not detected	Check cables and try again. if cables are good, possible bad hard disk.
Error initializing hard disk controller	Hard drive detected but cannot be read	May be a problem with a controller card. On IDE drives, it most likely is a problem with jumper settings.
Floppy disk controller error or no controller present	Floppy drive returned an error during POST	Check floppy cables to make sure they're properly seated and not backwards. If there are no floppy drives installed, be sure the Diskette Drive selection in setup is set to None.
Floppy disk(s) fail	Floppy drive returned an error during POST	Check floppy cables to make sure they're properly seated and not backwards. If there are no floppy drives installed, be sure the Diskette Drive selection in setup is set to None.
Hard disk initializing	Hard disk located and MBR is being read	Please wait for a moment.... Some hard drives require some extra time to initialize. May also indicate that there is an incorrect setting in the hard disk delay settings in CMOS.
HARD DISK INSTALL FAILURE	Undetermined hard disk error	Hard disk not detected. Check cables and jumper settings. If all are set correctly, possible bad drive.
Hard disk(s) diagnosis fail	SMART error returned	Check cables and run diagnostics. If error recurs, replace drive.
Keyboard error or no keyboard present	Keyboard returned an error during POST	POST detected no keyboard. Check cables and try again. Key may be stuck or the keyboard may be bad.

Error Message	Cause of Error	Possible Solution
Keyboard is locked out - Unlock the keyboard	Security setting	Lock on computer case is preventing the system from initializing the keyboard.
Memory address error at xxxxx	Bad memory	The address (in hexa-decimal) might tell you what RAM module is bad. Replace the memory.
Memory parity error at xxxxx	Bad memory	The address (in hexa-decimal) might tell you what RAM module is bad. Replace the memory.
Memory size has changed since last boot	Invalid memory configuration	System memory doesn't match the value stored in ESCD. Run setup and accept defaults.
Memory test	Not an error	Appears when a full memory test has been selected in startup options. Counts up the amount of memory tested.
Memory test fail	Bad memory	The address (in hexa-decimal) might tell you what RAM module is bad. Replace the memory.
Memory verify error at xxxxx	Bad memory	The address (in hexa-decimal) might tell you what RAM module is bad. Replace the memory.
No boot device was found	No drive with a valid MBR was located	Check cables and jumper settings. If all are set correctly, possible bad drive. Will also appear if hard disk is not formatted.
OFFENDING ADDRESS NOT FOUND	System cannot locate error	The message appears in conjunction with I/O CHANNEL CHECK and RAM PARITY ERROR messages when the system cannot identify the specific problem. Not much you can do about this one. If the problem persists, replace the motherboard.
OFFENDING SEGMENT: ...	System located error at named address	The message appears in conjunction with I/O CHANNEL CHECK and RAM PARITY ERROR messages after the system identifies the specific problem. Not much you can do about this one. If the problem persists, replace the motherboard.
Override enabled - Defaults loaded	CMOS factory defaults overriding custom settings	If CMOS configuration is incorrect or cannot be read, system loads factory defaults. Reset any necessary custom CMOS configuration settings.

continues

AWARD Text Messages (*continued*)

Error Message	Cause of Error	Possible Solution
PRESS A KEY TO REBOOT	An unrecoverable error has occurred	This message appears when an error occurs that requires you to reboot. Press any key to reboot the system
Press ESC to skip memory test	Not an error	Ummm. You press ESC and skip the memory test. How hard can it be?
PRESS F1 TO DISABLE NMI, F2 TO REBOOT	An NMI occurred during boot	BIOS has detected a nonmaskable interrupt condition during boot. Pressing F1 may allow you to bypass the NMI and continue to boot, or you can press F2 to reboot the system with the NMI enabled.
Press TAB to show POST screen	Clears splash screen	The splash screen covering the ugly blank display is also covering your POST messages. Press Tab to get rid of the splash screen.
Primary master hard disk fail	Primary master drive detected but could not initialize	The CMOS indicates a master drive is installed on the primary IDE port, but the drive is not responding. Go to the section on disk drives.
Primary slave hard disk fail	Primary slave drive detected but could not initialize	The CMOS indicates a slave drive is installed on the primary IDE port, but the drive is not responding. Go to the section on disk drives.
Resuming from disk, press TAB to show POST screen	Not an error	Indicates that the system is recovering from hibernation. Wait. You'll be able to use your computer eventually.
Secondary master hard disk fail	Secondary master drive detected but could not initialize	The CMOS indicates a master drive is installed on the secondary IDE port, but the drive is not responding. Go to the section on disk drives.
Secondary slave hard disk fail	Secondary slave drive detected but could not initialize	The CMOS indicates a slave drive is installed on the secondary IDE port, but the drive is not responding. Go to the section on disk drives.

Error Message	Cause of Error	Possible Solution
SYSTEM HALTED. (CTRL-ALT-DEL) TO REBOOT...	OS not detected	Generally indicates that no valid OS was detected. Can also result from failed memory or a corrupted MBR. Go to the section on disk drives.

Table 3.21

Dell BIOS System Messages

Error Message	Cause of Error	Possible Solution
nnnn cache RAM passed	Cache RAM passed POST diagnostics	None needed
nnnn extended RAM passed	Extended memory passed POST diagnostics	None needed
nnnn shadow RAM passed	Shadow memory passed POST diagnostics	None needed
nnnn system RAM passed	System memory passed POST diagnostics	None needed
CD-ROM drive identified	A CD-ROM drive has been detected and assigned a drive letter	None needed
Diskette drive A error; Diskette drive B error	The floppy disk drive failed diagnostics	Check drive cables to make sure they're seated properly and not backwards. Check the CMOS settings to make sure the correct drive type is identified. If all these are correct, replace drive.
Entering setup	The system is starting the system setup program	None needed
Extended RAM failed at offset: xxxxx	Memory modules in extended memory at the address identified in the offset failed diagnostics	Make sure the memory is properly seated, and that the CMOS is recognizing the correct amount of memory. If this fails, try replacing the memory modules.
Failing bits: nnnn	The n's represent the amount of memory that failed diagnostics	Make sure the memory is properly seated, and that the CMOS is recognizing the correct amount of memory. If this fails, try replacing the memory modules.

continues

Dell BIOS System Messages (*continued*)

Error Message	Cause of Error	Possible Solution
Fixed disk x failure; Fixed Disk controller failure	The hard disk (where x is replaced by the drive letter) did not respond to diagnostics	Check drive cables to make sure they're seated properly and not backwards. Check the CMOS settings to make sure the correct drive type is identified. If all these are correct, replace drive.
Fixed disk x identified	The system hard disk(s) have been properly identified and assigned a drive letter	None needed
Incorrect drive x type - Run setup	The floppy disk drive identified by POST does not match the configuration in CMOS	Check settings and reboot.
Invalid NVRAM media type	System can't read NVRAM (CMOS)	Clear the CMOS either by setting the jumper on the motherboard to Maintenance Mode, or by removing the system board battery for about sixty seconds. If it still can't read the factory defaults, flash a new BIOS.
Invalid system configuration data	The ESCD does not match the system configuration	Enter the system setup program and verify the system configuration, then restart the system.
Keyboard controller error	Keyboard did not respond to POST	Check keyboard cable to make sure it's properly seated. If still not recognized, try a different keyboard.
Keyboard error	Keyboard did not respond to POST	Check keyboard cable to make sure it's properly seated. If still not recognized, try a different keyboard.
Keyboard error nn	Stuck key on keyboard	nn represents the scan code. If you're a BIOS programmer, that tells you which key is stuck. If you're merely a computer tech, you'll have to get the cat off the keyboard and look for the stuck key.
Mouse initialized	A mouse was found on the system and properly initialized	None needed

Error Message	Cause of Error	Possible Solution
Operating system not found	Self-explanatory	If running NTFS and drive changes have been made, BOOT.INI might be pointing to the wrong drive. Also make sure there isn't a floppy in the disk drive.
Parity check 1 xxxxx	A parity error was detected at address xxxxx. If the address cannot be identified, the x's will be replaced by ?	Make sure the memory is properly seated, and that the CMOS is recognizing the correct amount of memory. If this fails, try replacing the memory modules.
Parity check 2 xxxxx	A parity error was detected at address xxxxx. If the address cannot be identified, the x's will be replaced by ?	Make sure the memory is properly seated, and that the CMOS is recognizing the correct amount of memory. If this fails, try replacing the memory modules.
Press <F1> to resume, <F2> to Setup	An error was detected, but the system can recover	F1 will continue the boot process, F2 will take you to CMOS setup.
Press <Del> to enter SETUP	Standard message displayed during POST	Ignore it if you just want to start the machine. Press the Delete key to enter CMOS setup.
Previous boot incomplete - Default configuration used	System detected the previous boot was unsuccessful	Due to an unsuccessful boot on the last attempt, the factory default settings were restored to the CMOS. If changes were made to the system, make sure they are reflected in the CMOS settings.

> For more information on CMOS Setup, go to page 118, Chapter 6 of *The Complete Guide to A+ Certification.*

Error Message	Cause of Error	Possible Solution
Real-time clock error	RTC reported invalid data during POST	Make sure the motherboard battery is good, set the time and date settings in CMOS setup and reboot.
Resource allocation conflict on motherboard	Plug 'n Play can't resolve all resources; conflict exists	Try swapping PCI slots between the offending device and another one. Check CMOS settings to make sure that there are no IRQs reserved that don't need to be.
Shadow RAM failed at offset: xxxxx	System was unable to read data from the memory at the specified address	Restore CMOS settings to factory defaults and reboot. If the error recurs, run diagnostics and look for bad memory.

continues

Dell BIOS System Messages (*continued*)

Error Message	Cause of Error	Possible Solution
System battery is dead - Replace and run SETUP	Just what it says	Buy a new battery, restore your CMOS configuration, and reboot.
System BIOS shadowed	BIOS shadowing was successful	None required.
System cache error - cache disabled	Cache RAM failed POST	This message is obsolete on most modern systems as cache is on the CPU. Which means if the error does occur, you'll be in the market for a new CPU.
System CMOS checksum bad - run SETUP	Either you entered an invalid CMOS configuration, or it has become corrupt	Try restoring to factory defaults. If this fails, flash a new copy of the BIOS.
System RAM failed at offset: xxxxx	POST returned an error when checking system RAM; xxxxx's mark the spot	Make sure the memory is properly seated and that the CMOS is recognizing the correct amount of memory. If this fails, try replacing the memory modules.
System timer error	The timer test failed	This message may mean a failed motherboard. But it can also point to a corrupt BIOS. Reset to factory defaults and try again. If the error recurs, it is likely time for a new motherboard.

Table 3.22

Phoenix BIOS Text Error Messages

Error Message	Cause of Error	Possible Solution
Diskette drive A error	Floppy drive failed POST	Floppy drive could not be initialized. Check cables and try again. If no floppy is installed, set the CMOS accordingly.
Extended RAM failed at offset: xxxxx	Memory failure	System can't read extended memory. Check CMOS settings and try again.
Failing Bits: xxxxx	Memory failure	POST returned an error during the memory check. xxxxx reports the failing address. Replace the defective module.

Error Message	Cause of Error	Possible Solution
Fixed disk 0 failure	Primary master IDE drive not initialized	Check the cables and jumper settings. Make sure the CMOS settings are correct.
Fixed disk 1 failure	Primary slave IDE drive not initialized	Check the cables and jumper settings. Make sure the CMOS settings are correct.
Fixed disk controller failure	Hard disk controller failure	Check the cables and jumper settings. Make sure the CMOS settings are correct. Make sure no user-configured device is conflicting with the hard disk controller.
Incorrect drive A: type - Run setup	Floppy drive type mismatch	Check the CMOS settings to make sure they match the installed drive.
Invalid NVRAM media type	CMOS can't be read	Set back to factory defaults and try again. If this fails, flash a new BIOS.
Keyboard controller error	Keyboard controller failure	Check cable. If that's not it, replace keyboard.
Keyboard error	Keyboard didn't respond to POST	Check cable. If that's not it, replace keyboard.
Keyboard error nn	Stuck key	Get the cat off the keyboard and check for stuck keys.
Keyboard locked - Unlock key switch	Case lock is locked	Keyboard is disabled until keylock is disabled.
Monitor type does not match CMOS - Run setup	Display settings incorrectly configured	Monitor type not correctly identified in setup.
Operating system not found	Just what it says	Check the floppy drive for disks. Check the CMOS settings to make sure the correct boot sequence is configured. Run diagnostics on the hard disk. Make sure you've actually installed an OS.
Parity check 1	Memory failure	Parity error found in the system bus. BIOS attempts to locate the address and display it on screen. If it cannot locate the address, it displays ???
Parity check 2	Memory failure	Parity error found in the I/O bus. BIOS attempts to locate the address and display it on screen. If it cannot locate the address, it displays ???

continues

Phoenix BIOS Text Error Messages (*continued*)

Error Message	Cause of Error	Possible Solution
Press <F1> to resume, <F2> to setup	Standard message after detecting a previously failed boot	Displayed after any recoverable error message. Press F1 to start the boot process or F2 to enter setup and change any settings.
Real-time clock error	RTC chip returned invalid information	Check the battery, reset time and date, and reboot.
Shadow RAM failed at offset: xxxxx	BIOS was unable to copy to RAM	May indicate bad memory or it may indicate corrupted BIOS. Flash a new BIOS and try again. If that fails, run diagnostics on the RAM.
System battery is dead - Replace and run setup	Please tell me I don't have to explain this one!	Do what the message says.
System cache error - Cache disabled	POST detected an error in L2 cache	On newer systems this is an obsolete message. Refers to L2 cache installed on the system board. Modern CPUs have L2 cache on-chip. If you get this message, it most likely means you're replacing your CPU. While you're at it, get a MAC.
System CMOS checksum bad - Run setup	CMOS can't be read	Set back to factory defaults and try again. If this fails, flash a new BIOS.
System RAM failed at offset: xxxxx	Memory failure	POST returned an error during the memory check. xxxxx reports the failing address. Replace the defective module.
System timer error	The timer test failed	Requires repair of system motherboard.

Table 3.23

Numerical Error Messages at Startup

The text messages listed above are commonly known as the verbose error messages. It is far more common to have numerical error messages appear on the screen. There is nothing more satisfying first thing in the morning than seeing the message "ERROR 10" appear on your screen with no further explanation than that. Well, perhaps a large black coffee and a bagel with cream cheese and chives.

Now there is nothing I would like more than to include charts of all the number codes you're likely to see. Herein lies the problem. With each BIOS manufacturer, the number codes change with each version. For example, with AMI, error code 08 means either "Delta counter channel 2 initialization complete," "8042 keyboard controller tested," or "CMOS initialization," depending on which version of the BIOS you have. To make matters worse, the messages have been known to alternate within revisions of the same version! If I include all of those charts, this book would hardly fit in your pocket. Therefore, I'm going to have to refer you to the manufacturers' Web sites for translating numerical codes. Most manufacturers have a support site with links to specific BIOS versions. Sorry I can't be more specific.

Part 4

Disk Drives

There is probably no device in a computer system that occupies more of the technician's time than the disk drives. Typical computers contain at least three different drives; many contain more than that. At the least, the average PC holds a floppy diskette drive, a hard disk drive, and some form of optical drive — CD-ROM, CD-RW, or DVD. A large percentage of machines these days have two hard disks and an even greater percentage have two optical drives. Managing and maintaining these drives is key to keeping a system at peak performance.

Floppy Diskette Drives

As complicated as they are, floppy diskette drives (**Figure 4.1**) are one of the simpler devices in a computer system. Still, they are a mechanical device, subject to wear, tear, and abuse. A floppy drive has a lot of different parts, but here are the key ones for the technician to consider:

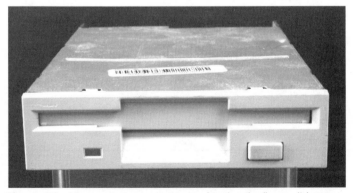

Figure 4.1 Many systems are starting to abandon the floppy diskette as obsolete. I'll lose mine when there is a bootable medium other than the floppy that lets me flash a BIOS on every system manufactured.

✔ A *clamping mechanism* holds the diskette in place as it spins.

✔ A *spindle motor* spins the diskette.

✔ One or two *magnetic read/write (R/W) heads* are mounted on an actuator arm that moves the heads over the surface of the medium. The initial read/write head is positioned to read the bottom surface of the diskette.

✔ A *head actuator* positions the R/W heads at the appropriate track and sector on the diskette.

✔ A *sensor* detects the rotational position of the diskette. 5.25" drives use an index hole cut in the sleeve, while there is a magnetic sensor in 3.5" drives.

Over time, there have been three sizes of floppy disk. The original, and long since obsolete, disk was 8" across and held 160KB. Since the advent of the PC there have been 5.25" floppy disks and 3.5" floppy diskettes (**Table 4.1**). 5.25" versions are now obsolete as well, but enough vintage computers still contain this drive that I will include them for reference.

For more information on The Floppy Disk, go to page 262, Chapter 12 of *The Complete Guide to A+ Certification.*

Floppy Disk(ette) Formats, Past and Present

5.25" Format

Specification	Double Density	High Density
Bytes per sector	512	512
Sectors per track	9	15
Tracks per side	40	80
Tracks per inch	48	96
Number of sides	2	2
Capacity	360K	1.2MB
Track width	.33mm	.16mm
Default cluster size	1	2
FAT length (sectors)	2	7
Root directory length (sectors)	7	14
Total sectors per disk	720	2400

3.5" Format

Specification	Double Density	High Density (1.44MB)	2.88MB
Bytes per sector	512	512	512
Sectors per track	9	18	36
Tracks per side	80	80	80
Tracks per inch	135	135	135
Number of sides	2	2	2
Capacity	720K	1.44MB	2.88MB
Track width	.115mm	.115mm	.115mm
Default cluster size	1	2	2
FAT length (sectors)	3	9	9
Root directory length (sectors)	7	14	15
Total sectors per disk	720	2400	5760

Table 4.1: Specifications for 5.25" floppy disks and 3.5" floppy diskettes

The Cable

The cable has a 34-pin connector, usually keyed. On two-device cables, conductors 10 through 17 will be twisted around between the middle connector and the end (**Figure 4.2**). This assures that the device on the end will be the bootable device. The 34th conductor is the drive change indicator (**Figure 4.3**). If this conductor is broken or shorted, the OS will not know when the disk in the drive has been changed and will show the same directory on repeated reads.

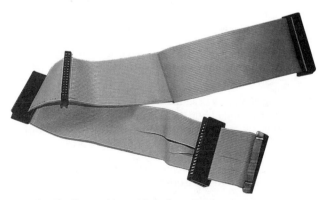

Figure 4.2 The floppy drive cable is the twisted one.

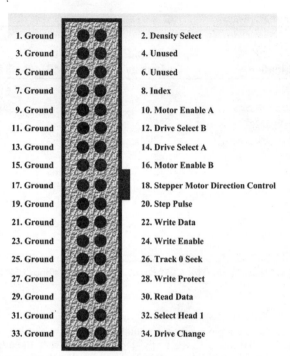

1. Ground	2. Density Select
3. Ground	4. Unused
5. Ground	6. Unused
7. Ground	8. Index
9. Ground	10. Motor Enable A
11. Ground	12. Drive Select B
13. Ground	14. Drive Select A
15. Ground	16. Motor Enable B
17. Ground	18. Stepper Motor Direction Control
19. Ground	20. Step Pulse
21. Ground	22. Write Data
23. Ground	24. Write Enable
25. Ground	26. Track 0 Seek
27. Ground	28. Write Protect
29. Ground	30. Read Data
31. Ground	32. Select Head 1
33. Ground	34. Drive Change

Figure 4.3   Pinouts for a floppy drive cable

Installing Floppy Diskette Drives

If you look at the back of a floppy drive (**Figure 4.4**), you will see a 34-pin connector for the data cable, a small round device (this is the power supply for the drive), and a smaller 4-pin power connector. While most drives are clearly labeled as to which of the pins represents pin number one, this isn't something you can easily see when the drive is installed in the system. Typically, the number one conductor goes to the inside, nearest the power supply.

Installing a floppy drive is as simple as mounting the drive into the drive bay, attaching the ribbon data cable in the correct orientation, plugging in the power cable, and firing the machine up. The vast majority of BIOS versions automatically detects the presence (or lack thereof) of a floppy diskette drive and auto-configure accordingly. If the drive does not get recognized on the first boot, you may have to go into CMOS setup and configure the drive (See **Figure 4.5**).

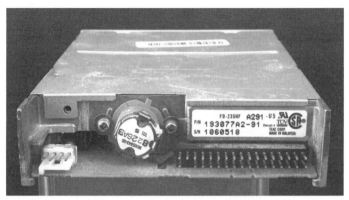

Figure 4.4 The back of a floppy disk drive

Figure 4.5 Even a modern BIOS such as this provides support for ancient drives, like the 360KB 5.25" drive. One of the options is to disable the drive.

Troubleshooting Floppy Drives

The vast majority of errors attributed to the floppy diskette drive are actually the fault of the diskette and not the drive. Still there are some errors attributable to the drive and/or cable. Sometimes it is even your BIOS. Common floppy drive problems are discussed in the list that follows.

Cable Problems

Repeating directories: You run a directory of a diskette to see what's on it. It doesn't have what you're looking for so you stick the next diskette in, and are presented with the same directory. The 34th conductor on the floppy cable being crimped or broken causes this. Replace the cable.

Drive not found, activity light stays on: The floppy drive cable is the one ribbon cable that is relatively easy to put on backwards. This is the symptom you will get. Reverse the cable on the drive.

Drive not found, POST does not activate drive: Check the data cable and the power cable. If either one is off or loose, the drive won't be detected during POST.

Diskette Problems

Data error reading drive A: While attempting to read the floppy diskette, the drive was unable to read one or more sectors. Run a disk repair utility and try again.

I/O error reading drive A: While attempting to read the floppy diskette, the drive was unable to read one or more sectors. Run a disk repair utility and try again.

Sector not found: While attempting to read the floppy diskette, the drive was unable to read one or more sectors. Run a disk repair utility and try again.

Invalid media type. Format diskette? An attempt to read either the boot sector or the file allocation tables (FAT) failed. Sometimes a disk repair utility will fix this. Usually the data is lost.

Not ready reading drive A: Usually this is because the disk is not fully inserted into the drive. Of course, I've *never* done that personally. Occasionally it results from a bad boot sector or FAT.

Drive Problems

General failure reading drive A: This is one of those problems that could easily fall under diskette problems as well. But I didn't have as many drive problems, so I wanted to equal it out. This problem can result from a disk drive that is not properly installed (e.g., the cables are loose or off, the drive is not properly configured in the CMOS, or it is disabled in the OS) or a diskette that has not yet been formatted.

For more information on Troubleshooting Floppy Disk Drives, go to page 267, Chapter 12 of *The Complete Guide to A+ Certification*.

Invalid drive specification: Perhaps you simply can't type. Typing DIR S: at the command prompt will not give you a directory of the A: drive. It can also be that the drive is not properly installed (see General failure reading drive A:) or that the drive has been disabled in the BIOS.

BIOS Problems

Floppy drive not found: Press F1 [or perhaps another key] to continue: This might be a cable issue, so check both the data ribbon cable and the power cable first. If those check out fine, see if the CMOS is configured for the wrong type of drive.

No error is reported, but the drive is not available after boot: Check for two things in the CMOS settings. First of all, is there a floppy drive configured at all? If the floppy drive settings in CMOS says NONE or DISABLED, then that's probably a very good reason you're not seeing one after boot. Second, check your version of BIOS for a collection of security settings. It may be disabled there.

Hard Disk Drives

Hard disk drives in modern computers are typically IDE, SCSI, or Serial ATA (SATA). Each drive type has its own peculiarities and offers different challenges to the technician. The following sections will help you muddle through the process of installing and troubleshooting hard disk drives.

Identifying the Drive Type

The three different drive types each have different physical characteristics that help make it easier to identify what kind of drive you're holding in your hands. Suffice it to say that you won't have much luck trying to plug a SCSI drive onto an IDE cable. Configuring them is different as well.

IDE Drives

The back of an IDE drive (**Figure 4.6**) will feature a 40-pin connector for the data cable, a 4-pin power connector with beveled edges, and a series of jumpers. The data connector is keyed so that you can't possibly plug the cable in backwards unless you're King Kong. The same is true of the power connector, due to the beveled edges. Jumper settings vary with the manufacturer. There is a section on that subject later in this Part.

For more information on Hard Drive Interfaces, go to page 314, Chapter 14 of *The Complete Guide to A+ Certification.*

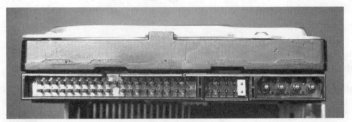
Figure 4.6 The back of an IDE hard disk drive

IDE Jumper Settings

As different brands have different jumper settings, and a picture is worth a thousand words (especially in the case of showing jumper settings), I have taken the most common brands and provided illustrations of jumper settings for standard installations in the next several figures.

Fujitsu Drives

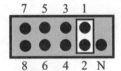
Figure 4.7 Fujitsu drives, Master device

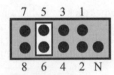
Figure 4.8 Fujitsu drives, Slave device

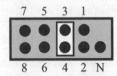
Figure 4.9 Fujitsu drives, Cable Select device

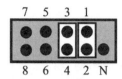

Figure 4.10 Fujitsu drives, Device active/Slave present

IBM Drives

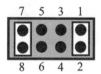

Figure 4.11 IBM/Hitachi drives, Master device

Figure 4.12 IBM/Hitachi drives, Slave device

Figure 4.13 IBM/Hitachi drives, Cable Select device

Maxtor Drives

Maxtor Drives have used three separate configurations over the years. These have been classified Style A, Style B, and Style C, and each type requires a different jumper setting. You wouldn't want it to be easy would you? Then everybody could do your job.

Maxtor, Style A

Figure 4.14   Maxtor drives, Style A Master device

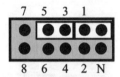

Figure 4.15   Maxtor drives, Style A Slave device

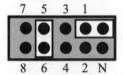

Figure 4.16   Maxtor drives, Style A Cable Select device

Maxtor, Style B

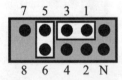

Figure 4.17   Maxtor drives, Style B Master device

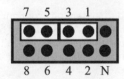

Figure 4.18   Maxtor drives, Style B Slave device

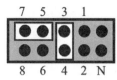

Figure 4.19 Maxtor drives, Style B Cable Select device

Maxtor, Style C

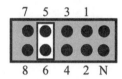

Figure 4.20 Maxtor drives, Style C Master device

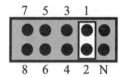

Figure 4.21 Maxtor drives, Style C Slave device

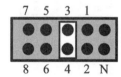

Figure 4.22 Maxtor drives, Style C Cable Select device

Seagate Drives

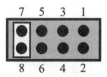

Figure 4.23 Seagate drives, Master device

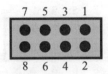

Figure 4.24   Seagate drives, Slave device

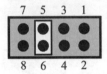

Figure 4.25   Seagate drives, Cable Select device

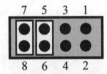

Figure 4.26   Seagate drives, Master/Non-ATA slave

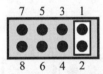

Figure 4.27   Seagate drives, Limit Drive Capacity

Western Digital Drives

Western Digital hard disks shipped in two styles. One style featured a
6-pin jumper, while the second style featured 10 pins. The following
are the jumper settings for standard installations of both styles.

Six-pin Configurations

Figure 4.28   Western Digital, 6-pin jumpers, Master

Figure 4.29 Western Digital, 6-pin jumpers, Slave

Figure 4.30 Western Digital, 6-pin jumpers, Cable Select

Ten-Pin Configurations

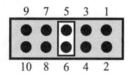

Figure 4.31 Western Digital, 10-pin jumpers, Master

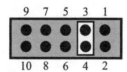

Figure 4.32 Western Digital, 10-pin jumpers, Slave

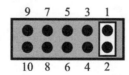

Figure 4.33 Western Digital, 10-pin jumpers, Cable Select

SCSI Drives

SCSI drives come in one of two types. Serial SCSI is self-configuring and therefore won't be discussed here, aside from a nodding acknowledgement. Parallel SCSI drives look very much like an IDE drive except they will have either a 68-pin D-sub or an 80-pin D-sub connector. Also, there will be more options for jumper settings, where jumpers are used.

SCSI devices are categorized as single-ended (SE) devices, high-voltage differential (HVD) devices, or low-voltage differential (LVD) devices. (For a more detailed discussion about these classifications, see *The A+ Guide to PC Hardware Maintenance and Repair*.) For the most part, different SCSI types cannot be mixed on the same SCSI chain. The exception is that multimode LVD (usually labeled LVD/SE) can detect the presence of SE devices on the chain and automatically switch to SE mode. Therefore,

For more information on How SCSI
Works, go to page 348, Chapter 15 of
The Complete Guide to A+ Certification.

devices will be marked as to what type they are with a simple diagram. **Figure 4.34** shows the diagrams used to label SCSI devices.

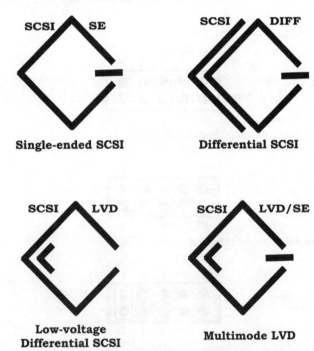

Figure 4.34   Labeling diagrams for SCSI devices

The next several illustrations and tables will show settings for some popular SCSI drives.

Fujitsu SCSI Drives

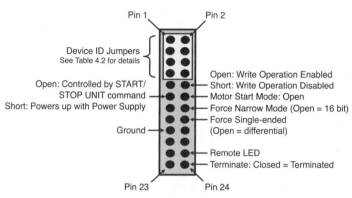

Figure 4.35 Jumper settings for Fujitsu SCSI drives

Jumper Placement for Fujitsu SCSI Device IDs

Pin 1-2	Pin 3-4	Pin 5-6	Pin 7-8	ID
Open	Open	Open	Open	0
Short	Open	Open	Open	1
Open	Short	Open	Open	2
Short	Short	Open	Open	3
Open	Open	Short	Open	4
Short	Open	Short	Open	5
Open	Short	Short	Open	6
Short	Short	Short	Open	7
Open	Open	Open	Short	8
Short	Open	Open	Short	9
Open	Short	Open	Short	10
Short	Short	Open	Short	11
Open	Open	Short	Short	12
Short	Open	Short	Short	13
Open	Short	Short	Short	14
Short	Short	Short	Short	15 (default)

Table 4.2

IBM SCSI Drives

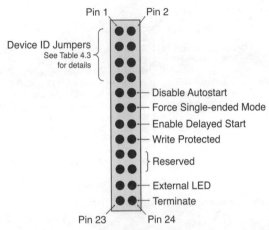

Figure 4.36 Jumper settings for IBM SCSI drives

Jumper Placement for IBM SCSI Drives

Pin 1-2	Pin 3-4	Pin 5-6	Pin 7-8	ID
Open	Open	Open	Open	0
Open	Open	Open	Short	1
Open	Open	Short	Open	2
Open	Open	Short	Short	3
Open	Short	Open	Open	4
Open	Short	Open	Short	5
Open	Short	Short	Open	6
Open	Short	Short	Short	7
Short	Open	Open	Open	8
Short	Open	Open	Short	9
Short	Open	Short	Open	10
Short	Open	Short	Short	11
Short	Short	Open	Open	12
Short	Open	Short	Short	13
Short	Short	Open	Short	14
Short	Short	Short	Short	15

Table 4.3

Maxtor SCSI Drives

Atlas 15K Series II

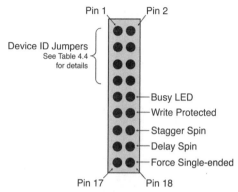

Figure 4.37 Maxtor 15K Series II jumper settings

Jumper Placement for Maxtor 15K Series II Drives

Pin 1-2	Pin 3-4	Pin 5-6	Pin 7-8	ID
Open	Open	Open	Open	0
Short	Open	Open	Open	1
Open	Short	Open	Open	2
Short	Short	Open	Open	3
Open	Open	Short	Open	4
Short	Open	Short	Open	5
Open	Short	Short	Open	6
Reserved for Host Adapter				7
Open	Open	Open	Short	8
Short	Open	Open	Short	9
Open	Short	Open	Short	10
Short	Short	Open	Short	11
Open	Open	Short	Short	12
Short	Open	Short	Short	13
Open	Short	Short	Short	14
Short	Short	Short	Short	15 (default)

Table 4.4

Atlas 15K

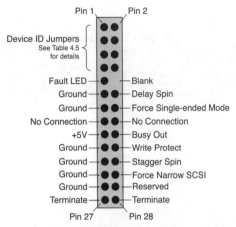

Figure 4.38   Maxtor 15K jumper settings

Jumper Placement for Maxtor 15K Drives

Pin 1-2	Pin 3-4	Pin 5-6	Pin 7-8	ID
Open	Open	Open	Open	0
Short	Open	Open	Open	1
Open	Short	Open	Open	2
Short	Short	Open	Open	3
Open	Open	Short	Open	4
Short	Open	Short	Open	5
Open	Short	Short	Open	6
Reserved for Host Adapter				7
Open	Open	Open	Short	8
Short	Open	Open	Short	9
Open	Short	Open	Short	10
Short	Short	Open	Short	11
Open	Open	Short	Short	12
Short	Open	Short	Short	13
Open	Short	Short	Short	14
Short	Short	Short	Short	15 (default)

Table 4.5

Seagate SCSI Drives

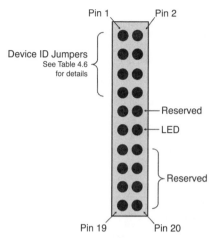

Figure 4.39   Seagate SCSI jumper settings

Jumper Placement for Seagate SCSI Drives

Pin 1-2	Pin 3-4	Pin 5-6	Pin 7-8	ID
Open	Open	Open	Open	0
Short	Open	Open	Open	1
Open	Short	Open	Open	2
Short	Short	Open	Open	3
Open	Open	Short	Open	4
Short	Open	Short	Open	5
Open	Short	Short	Open	6
Short	Short	Short	Open	7
Open	Open	Open	Short	8
Short	Open	Open	Short	9
Open	Short	Open	Short	10
Short	Short	Open	Short	11
Open	Open	Short	Short	12
Short	Open	Short	Short	13
Open	Short	Short	Short	14
Short	Short	Short	Short	15 (default)

Table 4.6

Troubleshooting Hard Drives

Problems with hard drives will fall under one of two categories. They

For more information on Troubleshooting
Hard Drives, go to page 340, Chapter 14 of
The Complete Guide to A+ Certification.

either don't work at all, or they seem to work when you start the machine, but they're acting up in some way, shape, or form. I'll cover both bases.

When the Drive Isn't Seen

If the drive isn't being seen at all by the system, nine times out of ten, it's a configuration issue. You boot the machine and all you have is drive A. You might know this is happening right off the bat if you get error messages like, "No Fixed Disk Present," "Hard Disk Controller Failure," or any one of several numeric error messages in the 17xx range, including 1701, 1780, 1781, 1790, and 1791. Other error messages that point to this include "Hard Disk Configuration Error," "Hard Disk 0 Failure," or "Invalid Drive Specification."

Ask this question: Was this drive just installed, or has it been in place for a while? If you just installed it, check the following:

✔ **Is the power connector (Molex) hooked up?** Drives have a tendency to not work as well when there is no electricity coming to them.

✔ **Check the Molex to make sure there's current coming through it.** This is where having a multimeter comes in handy.

✔ **Did you use a Y-cable to get power to the drive?** If so, try hooking it up directly to one of the cables coming straight out of the power supply. The Y-connector might be bad.

✔ **Is the ribbon cable connected?** Even if there's power going to the drive, the BIOS finds the drive on POST by sending signals down the cable. No cable, no signals. No signals, no drive.

✔ **Is the ribbon cable connected to the proper port on the motherboard or I/O card?** On older machines, it was necessary for the boot drive to be on the primary port, or it wouldn't be recognized.

✔ **Check the jumpers for Master/Slave if it is an IDE drive.** If the settings are right, check and see if you have a Cable Select (CS) cable. Those can drive you nuts, too. A notch clipped out of the 28th conductor tells you it is CS, but not seeing a notch doesn't necessarily tell you it isn't. To be on the safe side, put the master drive in the middle connector and the slave on the end.

✔ **Check device ID numbers on SCSI drives.** Two devices can't share the same ID unless they're part of an array.

✔ **Check your CMOS settings.** On many machines, it's possible to disable the IDE ports. Maybe the IDE port got disabled somehow. If the CMOS thinks there isn't a drive there, nothing else matters. The drive isn't there. On most machines, the default is "AUTO," so this shouldn't be an issue. But people do play with CMOS settings, even though they should know better.

✔ **Is the drive any good?** Hey, face it! Sometimes, you just get a bad drive. Make it the only device on the primary IDE port, set it to master, put it in the middle connector, make sure it's got power, and fire it up. Still not there? You might have a bad drive, but you also might have a bad port. Try a drive you know works.

When the Drive Is There, More or Less

While booting the machine, the POST routine usually displays its progress. On some brands of computer, these messages are concealed by the manufacturer's logo. You need to disable this screen if possible. The POST messages can contain information that helps with trouble-shooting certain problems. Press the <Esc> key as soon as the promo screen appears, and you should see the POST messages. Usually. One of the messages displayed is a listing of IDE devices found.

If you can't clear that screen, or are a little late on the uptake, you should also get a message telling you what key to press to enter the CMOS setup program. There's a table that might help you figure this out in Part 3, Motherboard Components. Many BIOS products have an IDE Autodetect utility that will tell you if it's finding a drive or not. Run that.

If the machine makes it all the way through the POST routine and then fails, there are several things to look at:

✔ **Is the hard drive recognized by the BIOS, but not the operating system?** Check the following:
   • Are the installation parameters set correctly?
   • Does your BIOS support the type of drive you're using? This is mostly a problem on older machines.

✔ **Are you using the correct translation mode?** If the CMOS somehow got accidentally moved from LBA to Large or Normal, the OS is going to choke.

✔ **Did somebody accidentally FDISK or format the drive?** Fix the problem, then take the machine away from the user!

✔ **Did you get an error message saying "I/O error reading Drive C:"?** This could be a bad thing. Many viruses attack the boot sector, and this is the message you're likely to get. Most reliable antivirus programs, such as McAfee or Norton AntiVirus, provide a bootable diskette that starts machines that are so affected. Maybe you'll get lucky and that can fix the problem. Then again, maybe you won't. If you prepared the drive using one of Microsoft's versions of FDISK, use that same version and try the command FDISK /MBR. That can sometimes repair a corrupted master boot record. That same error message can result from a damaged boot sector. If this is the case, the drive is dead. It might be possible to salvage the data from the drive.

✔ **Did you get the message "No Operating System Found"?** If this happens, take that boot diskette you made earlier and boot to the A:\ prompt. Now log onto the C: drive by typing C:\ and pressing the <Enter> key. If you get a C:\ prompt, type CD WINDOWS or CD DOS depending on what you're using for an OS. Does your prompt change to C:\WINDOWS? If it does, it's unlikely you have a bad drive, but rather a corrupted installation of your OS. Before you get rash and FDISK the drive and start over, try reinstalling the OS over the previous installation. That way you don't blow away all of your other directories. Most of your data can be salvaged, although you will probably have to reinstall most, if not all, of your applications.

✔ **Does your machine boot okay, but Windows always has to start a ScanDisk?** This could be a sign of impending drive failure. Is ScanDisk finding a lot of bad sectors? If so, back up your data and replace the drive now, while you still have your data intact.

✔ **Do you get the message "Invalid Command Interpreter," "No Boot Device Available," or "Missing Operating System"?** These usually indicate that the MBR has become corrupted. Try the FDISK /MBR command (which only occasionally works) or use one of several third-party utilities that are available for restoring MBRs.

✔ **Do you get the message "General Failure Reading Drive C:" either on bootup or long after the system boots, while you're running an application?** This indicates bad sectors on the drive. Run ScanDisk. Boot to a floppy and run it from there, if necessary.

Since hard drives have become so incredibly cheap (relatively speaking), it is becoming easier for an IT administrator to take a hard drive exhibiting any of the above symptoms, especially a drive that announces bad sectors, and circular file it, replacing it with a new drive. In a mission-critical installation, it is probably not a bad idea to replace the drive, but you might want to try something before you are too quick to throw away what might be a perfectly good drive.

Sometimes, the operating system has a hard time reading a particular cluster, so it relocates the cluster and marks it bad. That is a safety net programmed into the OS to protect your data. The cluster might not necessarily be bad, however. There may have simply been a temporary problem. Shutting down a system while the OS is still running can do that.

So before you discard the drive, FDISK it, format it, and put it to use in a less critical installation. It might continue to work for years.

When the Drive Does Not Format to Capacity

A problem that is gradually working its way out of modern installations occurs when a larger hard drive is installed, and then only formats to a fraction of its capacity. Years ago, it was possible to have your drive format to 508MB, regardless of how large it was. This was because the BIOS and/or chipset on the motherboard only supported the first generation of IDE devices. If it was just the BIOS that was the issue, the problem could be solved by installing an I/O card equipped with ATA-3 or later IDE, as long as it was equipped with supplemental BIOS. If the chipset was the limitation, the only solution was a new motherboard.

Next came the 8GB limitation. If the BIOS and/or chipset did not support the Int13h extensions, then a 40GB drive might be easily identified by the system. But would only format to a maximum of 8GB. The problem and solution here was the same as described in the previous paragraph.

The problem most recently seen is a 32GB limitation. Once again, this may be a BIOS limitation. If the BIOS version is prior to 1998, this is most likely the problem. Once again, an adapter card with supplemental BIOS may fix the problem as long as it's not inherent in the chipset. If your BIOS version is after 1999, it's most likely an OS-related issue. Windows 2000 and XP will only allow FAT32 partitions of 32GB. If you require a larger partition using those operating systems, you need to use the NTFS file system.

Optical Drives

You don't have to be all that old to be able to remember when the only optical drive on your computer was a standard CD-ROM drive. And you were considered somewhat affluent to own one of those. These days there are literally dozens of options. Each drive type has its own idiosyncrasies to deal with, but for some, the hard part is simply understanding what it is that's installed in the machine.

For more information on The Components of Multimedia, go to page 140, Chapter 17 of *The Complete Guide to A+ Certification*.

Identifying the Drive

Optical drives will be categorized by their speed, the type of media they are capable of reading, and finally by whether they are read-only devices, recordable devices, or rewritable devices. All optical drives carry speed ratings, and speed ratings can be very confusing, so I'll address all of these factors in the context of speed.

Speed Ratings for Optical Drives

From the outset, it looks like all speed ratings for optical drives are alike. They all have a number followed by an X. Unfortunately, what that number means varies, depending on whether you are looking at a CD drive (or variation on the theme) or a DVD drive.

CD-ROM and Recordable CD Drives

The earliest CD-ROM drives received their speed ratings based on the 150KB/sec transfer rate of the original CD-ROM for the PC. Therefore, a 2x CD-ROM transfers 300KB/s and an 8x CD-ROM transfers about 1200KB/s. Write speeds for recordable models are measured in the same manner. **Table 4.7** shows various speed ratings of CD drives.

Drives that are capable of recording new media have come in two types over the years. A conventional Compact Disk Recordable, or CD-R, can write data once to a disk, but cannot erase data. CD Rewritable (CD-RW) drives can read, write, and erase data. Therefore the CD-R drives feature two speeds, and the CD-RW drives require the user to understand three different speed ratings. A CD-R listed as 32x/8x could read data from a conventional CD at 3600KB/s, just like a standard 32x CD-ROM, and could write to a CD-R disk at 8x speeds, or approximately 1200KB/s. A CD-RW rated at 48\40\16x reads back conventional CDs at 48x, records CD-Rs at 40x, and can record CD-RW disks at 16x.

Conventional CD-ROM Specifications, Past, Present, and Future

Speed	Classification	Actual Bytes per Second	Transfer Rate (KB/s)
1x	Single speed	153,600	150
2x	Double speed	307,200	300
4x	Quad	614,400	600
6x	Six speed	921,600	900
8x	Eight speed	1,228,800	1200
12x	Twelve speed	1,536,000	1500
16x	Sixteen speed	1,843,200	1800
24x	Twenty-four speed	2,457,600	2400
32x	Thirty-two speed	3,686,400	3600
40x	Forty speed	4,915,200	4800
48x	Forty-eight speed	7,372,800	7200
56x	Fifty-six speed	8,601,600	8400

Table 4.7: CD-ROM speeds are all derived from the original 150KB/s speed of the first model of drive to be released.

DVD Drives

The world of DVD drives gets much more convoluted. There are several different data formats and technologies and not all are mutually compatible. Some formats were designed with audio-video (AV) technology as the motivating force, while others were looked at as simply data storage devices. A drive that supports as many of the different technologies as possible is preferable. Different DVD formats include the following:

DVD-ROM: The standard AV format used by the movie industry to record movies using a compressed streaming video file, accompanied by a separate audio track. We just call them DVDs these days and most of us have a large collection cluttering up the living room.

DVD+R: A recordable format developed by a consortium of manufacturers led by Philips that records up to 4.7GB of data permanently to the disk. DVD+R Dual Layer records data in two different layers on the disk, for a total of 8.5GB of maximum storage potential.

DVD+RW: A recordable format developed by a consortium of manufacturers led by Philips that allows the user to record, erase, and re-record up to 4.7GB of data an indefinite number of times. DVD+RW Dual Layer records data in two different layers on the disk, for a total of 8.5GB of maximum storage potential.

DVD-R: A recordable format developed by a consortium of manufacturers led by Panasonic that records data permanently to the disk. While similar to DVD+R in approach and in data storage capacity, the file formats are not mutually compatible. DVD-R Dual Layer records two layer media.

DVD-RW: A recordable format developed by a consortium of manufacturers led by Panasonic that allows the user to record, erase, and re-record data an indefinite number of times. While similar to DVD+RW in approach, the file formats are not mutually compatible. DVD-RW Dual Layer records two layer media.

DVD-RAM: Typically housed in a cartridge, the DVD-RAM is a data-only format. It is not compatible with any of the other DVD file systems.

It sort of makes deciding between mocha java and cappuccino in the morning seem tame doesn't it? DVD speed ratings can get equally confusing as well. Even though the syntax of a DVD drive looks the same, the numbers don't mean the same thing. A 4x DVD is not transferring data at the same speed as a 4x CD-ROM. A 1x DVD is the equivalent of an 8x CD-ROM, or about 1200KB/s. Speeds are not exact increments either. It is possible to have a 2.5x DVD drive.

Most drives released today are multi-function drives. By that, I mean that you can buy a DVD-RW, DVD+RW, CD-R, CD-RW, CD-ROM drive. Mine has all of the above and even comes with a convenient cup holder.

Optical Drive Loading Mechanisms

Most optical drives currently manufactured utilize a tray-loading mechanism for inserting the disk. However, this isn't true for all drives. Loading mechanisms that have been used, past and present, fall into one of three types. They will be a tray, a caddy, or a slot. There are advantages and disadvantages to each. Each has it own little quirks, so understanding the differences can be important.

The tray is far and away the most common mechanism seen today. Its advantages are that it is the simplest to manufacture, and therefore the least expensive. On the other hand, the disk gets a lot of handling and, if loaded incorrectly into the tray, may get damaged.

The caddy gets a lot of use with multidisk changers, but has appeared in the past on a few single-disk drives. With the caddy, the disk must be inserted into a carrier (the caddy), which is inserted into the drive. Disks get the most protection in this manner. For the user, on the other hand, changing between disks is much more inconvenient.

The slot has become popular with some manufacturers, and many customers like them as well. With a slot-loading drive, the user simply inserts the disk into the slot and a loading mechanism draws the disk into the drive and seats it properly. When the user pushes the eject mechanism, the disk is pushed back out. Unfortunately, this approach puts the maximum amount of wear on the disk.

Troubleshooting Optical Drives

For the most part, unwell optical drives exhibit symptoms similar to those of hard drives, except that they generally will not prevent your computer from booting properly. Unlike the hard drive, an optical drive is totally dependent on software drivers to work right, so a majority of the problems you face are either configuration or software issues. There are a few things, however, that can drive you nuts. Because CD-ROMs, CD-RWs, and DVDs all exhibit the same hardware issues, the advice in the following section (except where I name a specific kind of drive)

For more information on Installing CD-ROM Drives, go to page 419, Chapter 17 of *The Complete Guide to A+ Certification.*

applies to any of the above. If the issue is unique to a type of optical drive, then it's more likely to be a software or driver issue. Some things to look for when troubleshooting optical drives include the following:

✔ **I just installed a new optical drive and my system doesn't recognize it.** Check your jumpers first. They're just like hard drives in that they need to be either master or slave. Everything I talked about in the section on hard drives holds true here as well.

✔ **I just installed a new optical drive and my system doesn't recognize it. I've checked all the jumper settings and they're correct, and I've even checked to see if I have a cable-select cable. I still can't make it work.** Check and see if the IDE port onto which you are trying to install it has been disabled. Some CMOS setup programs allow for the disabling of ports for security reasons or simply in order to reclaim the IRQ.

✔ **I just installed a new CD-RW and my system doesn't recognize it. I've checked all the jumper settings and they're correct, and I've even checked to see if I have a cable-select cable. I still can't make it work.** Some CD-RWs only work if they're the master drive on the port. Since most systems require the bootable drive to be on the primary port, the solution is to move the CD-RW to the secondary port and let it be the master of its domain.

✔ **My optical drive works fine in Windows, but when I restart in DOS mode, it disappears.** Like I said, optical drives are totally dependent on software drivers. Windows loads its own drivers from the registry. When you boot in DOS mode, you need an autoexec.bat and config.sys file, just like in the old days.

✔ **My optical drive letter keeps changing.** That probably means that you're also using some form of removable medium that hooks up either to the parallel port or a USB port. When that drive is present, the BIOS reassigns drive letters.

✔ **My CD-ROM won't read CD-Rs or CD-RWs.** This is usually only a problem with older drives, but there are a couple of things that can cause this problem. One is that the older CD-ROM isn't capable of reading a multisession table of contents. You need a drive that is "multisession compliant" to read the newer media. The second thing that could be causing the problem lies in the mechanism itself. Early models of CD-ROM expect a certain contrast between the pits and lands. They simply can't extract the data off the disk if the contrast is too subtle.

✔ **I'm getting an inordinately high number of I/O errors on disks that other computers have no problem with.** Try running one of those cleaning disks made specifically for optical drives. If the lens on the optical stylus gets dirty, this will happen. If this doesn't work, check your CMOS settings for the drive and make sure it is correct. Many optical drives only work in PIO mode. If the drive is on the same cable as your UDMA hard drive, it may be forcing the drive into UDMA mode. Next, check the IDE cable. It shouldn't be longer than 18", but many manufacturers cheat this length and ship 24" cables. While this usually doesn't cause major problems, it can. Finally, if bus mastering has been set up on your machine, make sure you have an optical drive that is bus mastering capable. Pretty much any newer drive should be able to handle it, but if you brought an older drive into service for any reason, this can become an issue.

✔ **My kid (dog, husband, wife, best friend, but never me) scratched up one of my most critical CDs and now my drive won't read it.** The best solution is to replace the disk. If this isn't possible, try smearing a little toothpaste onto the surface of the disk. Take a moistened soft cloth and, in a circular motion, buff the scratched surface. Never do this on the label side! Once you've done this, rinse the disk and dry it with a soft cloth. This doesn't always work, but it has saved many a disk that my kid (dog, husband, wife, best friend, but never me) scratched for me.

Troubleshooting CD and DVD Recorders

When a CD or DVD recorder is working properly it's a marvel of technology we just can't live without. However, when things go wrong, these things seem to take on the personality of a vampire. Worse yet, the errors they report always seem to be in a language of their own. Here is a brief rundown on problems you might encounter and some possible solutions.

The Recorder Is Not Recognized as a Recording Drive

There are several things that can cause this. One feature of optical drives is something called Auto Insert Notification (AIN). When you place a disk in the drive, the drive notifies the OS that a new disk has arrived, so things like Windows Explorer can update directory listings, or AutoRun can launch the appropriate files. Not all recording drives like AIN. In Device Manager, go to the drive properties and turn AIN off.

The OS treats recording drives as SCSI devices, even if they are IDE drives. As such, they depend on the Advanced SCSI Programming Interface (ASPI) for functional support. A lot of software products sold to provide advanced functions for creating your own disks load their own ASPI drivers. Don't let multiple programs load multiple versions of ASPI drivers. Along these same lines, many devices rely on the OS version of ASPI driver. A drive that is newer than your version of OS might be looking for a later version of ASPI driver. See if your OS manufacturer has any ASPI patches that might help.

Does your motherboard installation disk load its own bus-mastering drivers for the IDE interface? Perhaps that isn't as compatible as the manufacturer would like you to believe. Try reloading the Windows or Linux default bus mastering drivers.

Buffer Underrun

Since this is a problem almost exclusive to Windows, my discussion will be centered on that. These issues don't seem to occur in Linux. The cause of the problem is that data being recorded to the medium needs to transfer to the medium at a rather specific rate. Drives use an area of memory called the buffer to store data and then subsequently release it as required by the recording mechanism. If the drive is copying data faster than the computer is filling the buffer, the buffer empties. When this happens, your recording fails. Usually when this happens, it happens almost as soon as you start the recording process. There are a few things you can look at to stop this from happening.

Make sure you're not running lots of other resource-hungry programs while you're burning disks. Even though Windows is supposed to be a multitasking OS, this is one job where you want all the resources you have available concentrating on the task at hand. Close all programs except for the ones absolutely necessary to complete the job at hand. In most cases, this means everything except your burning software.

Reduce your recording speed. Maybe you just don't have sufficient RAM or CPU horsepower to burn disks at 48x. Sometimes simply changing brands of recording software solves this problem. Some software sets aside a second-level buffer in RAM that it uses to feed the disk's buffer. And keep in mind; just because a company is charging an arm, a leg, and your first-born child for their product doesn't necessarily mean that it is better. The product I use is an open-source freeware product that didn't cost a nickel, and the reason I changed over was that it solved the very issue I'm now discussing. I'm not allowed to tout specific brands and products in this book, but if you check out CDBurnerXP Pro at www.cdburnerxp.se, you'll find a description of the product I'm not supposed to mention.

CD Recording Capacity

The amount of data that can be stored on a disk, or its capacity, can vary with the medium and, to a certain extent, with the type of data being stored. Officially, using the specifications of the original CD-ROM drive, a CD could hold about 650MB of data. In terms of audio format (using WAV files), this equated to about 74 minutes of audio. However, as recording technology improved, so has capacity. There are now several different brands of disk with differently rated capacities. **Table 4.8** lists some that are currently available.

CD-R and CD-RW Media Capacity

Storage in Megabytes	Minutes of Audio Stored
650	74
700	80
790	90
870	99

Table 4.8: CD-R and CD-RW media are no longer restricted to the original limitations of CD-ROM specifications.

Even these limitations aren't etched in stone. If all conditions are met, it is possible to over-record conventional media by a small amount. For this to happen all four of the following conditions must be met.

✔ The media being used must support over-burning.
✔ The recording drive must support over-burning.
✔ The CD-burning software being used to create the disk must be up to the task.
✔ The drive in which the disk will eventually be read must be able to read disks beyond the rated capacity.

How can you figure out if all of this is true? Start with the drive. This is an all-or-none situation. A given brand of CD-RW drive can either over-burn or it can't. Next comes the burning software. Most early versions of even the prominent brands do not support capacities beyond 650MB. Even the newer high-capacity media are only recog-nized as 650MB disks. End of story. If you want to play this game, buy new software. Most of the newer applications and new versions of long-standing applications support over-burning. As with the drives, it either does or it doesn't.

Usually, the media isn't the problem. Almost every brand of blank disk manufactured is deliberately designed with surplus space. The trick is in knowing how much surplus space you have. Deliberately record a disk that is far and away longer than the medium is capable of storing. When the disk fills up, you will receive a track following error. Pay attention to how much data was copied before the error occurred. A value slightly under the stated value is where the medium can be safely used. This varies from brand to brand, so don't use the values you derive from one test on every brand that's out there.

The final condition is one that is frequently out of your control. And that is whether or not a particular CD-ROM drive can read the disk once you've created it. What's the good in making a disk nobody can read? However, just because a specific drive can't read your disk right now doesn't mean you can't fix that problem. Some drives allow you to update the firmware in the controller circuitry. This is sort of like flash-ing the BIOS on a motherboard, only it is specific to the drive.

Updating the Firmware on an Optical Drive

Not all drives allow you to update the firmware. The only way to find out if your drive has this capability is to check with the manufacturer. Most of them have this information on their Web sites in the support section. Once you have determined that you can update the firmware for your drive, pay close attention to the instructions. Some can be updated from Windows or Linux. Others can only be updated from a command prompt. If the procedure calls for the latter, be prepared to make a boot floppy.

The firmware update will be downloaded as an executable file. To run this file, adhere to the following instructions to the letter, even if the manufacturer doesn't say to do so.

✔ Close all other programs running on the system.
✔ Make sure AIN is turn OFF!
✔ Disable any power saver functions. Sometimes this process can take a while, and if your machine goes to sleep in the middle of an upgrade, your drive is now a paperweight.
✔ Make sure there are no disks in the drive.

For the most part, if you follow the above precautions, your firmware upgrade should go smoothly.

Part 5

Memory

Of all the components in your PC, none has more impact on system performance than does the amount of random access memory (RAM) that is installed. A PC technician is going to be called on to install new RAM and to troubleshoot problems with existing RAM. This section will cover the basic elements of understanding necessary to accomplish these tasks.

For the most part, my discussions are going to center around memory types, memory packaging, and diagnosing memory problems. As far as theory on how RAM works, check with *The A+ Guide to PC Hardware Maintenance and Repair*.

Memory Packaging

Memory modules that are installed in computers come in a variety of different packages. Almost everything used today is going to be some variation on the Dual Inline Pin Package (DIMM). However, some legacy systems make use of other packages, so I'll briefly discuss some older technology as well.

Dual Inline Pin Package (DIPP): Shown in **Figure 5.1**. While no longer used for memory, this chip still sees a lot of use in modern PCs. Many BIOS manufacturers use this package to store their products. Other types of firmware find their homes in DIPPs as well. I'll forgo any discussions of other places you might see DIPPs at work.

Single Inline Memory Module (SIMM): Shown in **Figure 5.2**. The SIMM had a long lifespan, starting with the old 386-based PCs and lasting well into the days of Pentium-class machines. As you can see in the illustration, this module is an edge-card device. The terminal strips on either side of the base connect to the same wire, so mirrored connections perform identical functions. SIMMs originally were released as 30-pin modules. Starting with the 486-class machines, the 72-pin module became prominent. 72-pin SIMMs are referred to as 32-bit memory because 32 bits of memory are transferred on each cycle.

For more information on The Packaging of Memory, go to page 183, Chapter 9 of *The Complete Guide to A+ Certification*.

Figure 5.1 The Dual Inline Pin Package doesn't see much use in the world of memory any more. Still, it's a popular package for BIOS chips, so you need to be able to recognize it.

Figure 5.2 The Single Inline Memory Module

Dual Inline Memory Module (DIMM): Shown in **Figure 5.3**. The DIMM looks, feels, tastes, and smells just like a bigger version of the SIMM. However, it differs in that the terminals on each side of the edge connector perform separate functions. There is an ever-growing range of varieties of DIMM. The first versions to be released were 168-pin modules. More recent memory types have called for more connections and now we have 184-pin DIMMs and 240-pin DIMMs as well. DIMMs are 64-bit memory. Some printers use a 100-pin variety of the DIMM module as well.

Small Outline DIMM (SO-DIMM): Shown in **Figure 5.4**. SO-DIMMs find their homes these days almost exclusively in laptop computers. However, in the years they've been on the market, they've appeared in printers, on video cards, and even on SCSI adapters. The first SO-DIMMs were 72-pin modules. For a long time 144-pin modules were the most common. Many of today's modern memory types ship on 200-pin SO-DIMMs.

Figure 5.3 The 168-pin module was the first type of DIMM to be released.

Figure 5.4 If you're changing memory in your laptop, there's a pretty good chance you'll have a close encounter with a SO-DIMM.

Micro-DIMMs: Very small devices, such as handheld computers, require very small components. Micro-DIMMs were built with these products in mind. Micro-DIMMs look very much like SO-DIMMs, except that they are smaller and thinner. They come in 172-pin and 200-pin varieties.

Memory Types

The type of memory your system supports has a significant impact on overall performance. Unfortunately, you can't just arbitrarily decide to slap a faster type of memory into your computer, hoping for enhanced performance. The chipset dictates the type of memory you can use. And since memory types also come in different form factors, this can be a factor as well. With all the hype thrown around concerning the advantages of this kind of memory over that, it sounds almost like there are a thousand types to choose from. There aren't. There only two types actively used on modern computers. There are just a thousand varieties of each of those two. There are some earlier technologies, however, that will appear on legacy computers as well as in some component devices. I will discuss those as well.

For more information on How Memory Works, go to page 174, Chapter 9 of *The Complete Guide to A+ Certification*.

Dynamic Random Access Memory (DRAM): This simply refers to the memory used in computers. All memory used is some form of DRAM.

Fast Page Mode (FPM): This was the type of memory used on the first IBM PC. It remained popular until shortly after the release of the 80486 CPU, when the faster CPU made FPM a bottleneck. FPM is not used on computers anymore, but it still sees use on adapters as buffer memory.

Extended Data Out (EDO): EDO was 10 to 15 percent faster than FPM simply because it reduced the number of clock cycles required to set up a memory I/O operation, and also increased by one the number of memory reads that could occur on each I/O operation. EDO was used on 486, Pentium, and Pentium II computer systems, on video cards, and as buffer memory for SCSI adapters.

Synchronous DRAM (SDRAM): SDRAM moved part of the memory control circuitry off the motherboard and onto the memory module, allowing the CPU to directly control the memory chips. This allowed the memory to be read once on each and every clock cycle of the front side bus. As such, memory was sold as PC-66 (for a 66MHz FSB), PC-100 (100MHz FSB) and PC-133 (133MHz FSB). There was also a PC-150, even though there was never a CPU with a 150MHz FSB. This memory was produced to meet the demands of hobbyists who took immeasurable glee in how far beyond the limits they could push their systems. While it was certainly possible to put faster rated memory onto slower systems, it isn't a good idea to put slower memory onto faster systems. This can result in intermittent lockup and booting problems. Also, different speeds of memory should not be mixed in a system. This can result in a dramatic increase in memory errors and fatal application errors. SDRAM is 64-bit memory.

Double Data Rate SDRAM (DDR): This is simply SDRAM that can perform two read or write operations on each clock cycle of the front side bus. It is not a different type of memory. In order for you to use it, however, you must have a chipset that supports it. Typically DDR memory ships on 184-pin DIMMs (although there were some companies who shipped DDR on 168-pin modules).

DDR2: This is an evolutionary step in the development of DDR. It uses 50 percent less voltage that DDR, so it consumes less power. It can also be divided into logical channels, with each channel going through a refresh rate at a different time. Its real claim to fame is that it presents four bits to the memory bus on each clock cycle, so data throughput is twice as fast. DDR2 is not backwardly compatible with conventional DDR and will not coexist with it on the same motherboard. But don't worry about accidentally installing it on a machine that only supports DDR. It uses a 240-pin DIMM.

Rambus: Rambus memory is a somewhat proprietary form of memory. It was originally going to be the only memory that the Pentium 4 CPU would read. Intel quickly realized that was a big mistake and released motherboards and chipsets for the P4 that supported DDR as well.

Rambus's big claim to fame is that it sports 400, 533, and 800MHz bus speeds. But the apparent advantage is lost to the fact that it only transfers 16 bits of data on each of its clock cycles. Rambus uses a 184-pin socket, but it is not compatible with the 184-pin socket used by DDR.

Error Correction Code

Every memory type manufactured experiences a certain percentage of memory errors. Error Correction Code (ECC) memory is a form of memory that can not only detect a memory error, it can also correct it on the fly. It does so by providing a few extra bits for each data transfer. On a 72-pin SIMM, a total of 4 bits were available for error correction code. On a DIMM module, there was a whole byte of data.

What are those extra bits used for? When ECC first reads data from its memory cells, it looks at the data as if it were a long binary number instead of data. The control circuitry performs a mathematical calculation on that data and stores the result in the ECC bits. On the receiving end, the same calculation is performed and the results are compared to the value stored in ECC. If the values don't match, the data package is sent again.

ECC memory, as you might imagine, is typically more expensive than standard RAM. Motherboards that support ECC generally have a provision in the BIOS for turning the feature off if you don't need it, or can't find ECC RAM.

Registered Memory

Registered memory is able to reduce the number of errors significantly by maintaining a buffer memory area on the chip itself where the data from a particular I/O operation is stored and compared before being transmitted to cache. This is all fine and good as far as data integrity is concerned, but performance takes a big hit as a result.

Typically registered SDRAM is used on servers and high-end workstations. If a motherboard calls for registered memory, don't bother trying to use any other kind. It's not like ECC, where you can turn the feature on or off at will.

Understanding Memory Modules

Some chipsets support more than one memory type. Different memory types are frequently available in a variety of modules, and, with a couple of notable exceptions, different memory packages support different

For more information on Module Sizes and Banks of Memory, go to page 190, Chapter 9 of *The Complete Guide to A+ Certification*.

memory types as well. **Table 5.1** lists module types along with the kinds of memory that could be found on them.

Memory Types and Memory Modules

Memory Package	Memory Type	CPU Supported
30-pin SIMM	FPM	8088 – 80486
72-pin SIMM	FPM, EDO	80386-Pentium II
168-pin DIMM	FPM, EDO, SDRAM	80486 to Pentium III
184-pin DIMM	DDR	Pentium 4
184-pin RIMM	Rambus	Pentium 4
200-pin DIMM	Buffered SDRAM, DDR	Pentium 4
240-pin DIMM	DDR2	Pentium 4
72-pin SO-DIMM	FPM, EDO	80486-Pentium II
144-pin SO-DIMM	EDO, SDRAM	Pentium – Pentium III
200-pin SO-DIMM	DDR, DDR2	Pentium 4

Table 5.1: While not totally conclusive, this table lists the most common combinations of memory type and memory packaging seen over the past few years.

Understanding Memory Speed Ratings

Here's a typical scene for you. A man and wife walk into the computer store. He says, "I need a 512MB module for my Ultra-Micro 4.2GHz PC." She is impressed. The salesperson asks, "Do you need PC-2700 or PC-3200, and do you need CL2 or CL3?" I hate it when that happens, don't you?

While there are several factors that control memory speed, only two are anything you'll have to understand. CAS Latency (CL) is one of those factors, and bus speed is the other. I mentioned in Part 2 that CL timing was a significant factor to look at when tweaking the BIOS. If your motherboard supports CL2 memory, you should use it. You can use CL3 memory with no ill effects other than a hit in performance, but CL2 memory isn't that much more expensive and can boost total system performance by as much as 15 percent. Just make sure that, if you're replacing CL3 RAM with CL2, you swap out all your memory. Don't mix the types on the same motherboard. Also, after installing the new memory, go into the CMOS setup and make sure that the Advanced Chipset configuration is set for CL2 memory. The factory default is generally CL3.

Bus speed is the other factor you must consider. You need to match the bus speed of your memory to that of your motherboard. Once again, faster memory will work fine on a slower motherboard, but not vice versa. And don't mix and match bus speeds of memory on the same system. If you insist on overclocking your system bus, make sure you have the proper memory. With the older style SDRAM, it was fairly easy to understand the bus speeds. They were part of the memory rating. DDR gets a bit more complicated, because it uses overall data throughput as its rating. **Table 5.2** lists some common memory types, along with bus speed and average data throughput.

Speed Ratings of Memory

Rating	Bus Speed	Data Throughput
PC-66 SDRAM	66MHz	528Mb/s
PC-100 SDRAM	100MHz	800Mb/s
PC-133 SDRAM	133MHz	1064Mb/s
PC-150 SDRAM	150MHz	1200Mb/s
PC-1600 DDR	100MHz	1600Mb/s
PC-2100 DDR	133MHz	2100 Mb/s
PC-2700 DDR	166MHz	2700 Mb/s
PC-3200 DDR	200MHz	3200 Mb/s
PC-3500 DDR	266MHz	3700 Mb/s
PC2-3200 DDR2	200MHz	3200Mb/s
PC2-4200 DDR2	266MHz	4300Mb/s
PC2-5300 DDR2	333MHz	5300Mb/s

Table 5.2: Comparison of actual bus speeds and data throughput of different memory types

System Performance vs. Physical Memory Capacity

It has long been noted that the amount of memory installed in a machine has as much, if not more impact on system performance than CPU speed. In terms of raw CPU speed, it requires a doubling of actual clock speed to attain a 15 percent increase in overall system performance. A 15 percent boost is barely noticeable to the human user.

Crucial Memory Corporation, a key manufacturer of memory products, performed a series of tests related to the impact of RAM quantities on system performance. In these tests, they set up a Web server and bombarded it with requests. The speed at which the server could process requests increased dramatically with increased memory. **Table 5.3** lists the results of their tests.

Effect of Memory on System Performance[1]

Memory Installed	Latency (ms)	Increase over 512MB	Increase over 2GB
512MB	1199.410	N/A	N/A
2GB	600.785	49.91%	N/A
4GB	115.142	90.40%	80.83%

[1] Tests performed by VeriTest and commissioned by Crucial and reported on Crucial's Web site at http://support.crucial.com/library/server_memory_benchmark_tests.asp

Table 5.3: When you compare these results to the 15 percent boost you get from doubling CPU speed, a memory upgrade seems something of a bargain, doesn't it?

However, before you rush out and stock up on lots of memory, look at the applications you're going to be running as well as your system's OS. If you're running an old Windows 98 box, that OS had a built-in limitation of 64MB that that kernel processes could use. Applications, on the other hand, such as Adobe's Photoshop or PageMaker, could make use of as much RAM as you could throw at them. Win2K and WinXP have no such limitations that have been documented.

Troubleshooting Memory

When memory begins to fail, trying to figure out what is wrong can literally drive you nuts. Understanding how memory works and being able to figure out the problems it may cause are two different issues altogether. A big problem is that a number of symptoms that sick computers exhibit can indicate memory, CPUs, or motherboards. Also, memory problems are frequently intermittent. Which basically means they'll never show their face in the presence of a technician. Do yourself a favor and develop a systematic approach to all troubleshooting.

For more information on Troubleshooting Memory, go to page 195, Chapter 9 of *The Complete Guide to A+ Certification.*

With memory, you can start with the fact that there are three basic guises in which memory errors generally appear.

Memory Not Detected

One of the first diagnostics run by the POST program is a memory test. Failure to detect memory during POST can happen in two different ways. Each failure has a different impact on the boot process. If the system finds no memory at all, the speaker will emit a series of beeps and the boot process will halt. The other situation is when the system finishes the boot process successfully, but reports an amount of memory you know to be incorrect.

If the machine is unable to boot, analyze the situation a step at a time. Is this the first time a new computer has ever been turned on? If so, first check and see if the manufacturer installed any memory. Don't laugh! It's rare, but it happens.

If there are memory chips installed, make sure they are properly seated. If they're not, don't automatically call the company and start screaming. SIMM and DIMM modules alike sometimes come loose due to the rigors of ground shipping. Simply reseat the memory and try again. If the memory is securely seated and still not working, it is possible that you have a bad module.

What if you're trying to diagnose an older machine that's been around a while? The first thing to do is to try and figure out what, if anything, changed since the last time the computer worked properly. Was service recently done on the computer? Maybe the memory got knocked loose. It can happen.

Perhaps you just completed a memory upgrade and things aren't working as planned. If the machine was working fine before attempting the upgrade there are a couple of things to look at. Once again, is all the memory seated properly in the sockets? Mounting memory into sockets is not always as easy as the makers of boards would have you believe, especially if they used lower grade sockets. Run your fingers along the top edge of the modules. If there is more than one, then the edges should be perfectly parallel. If one seems to be either tipping or sinking, it isn't seated. Try again. If any of the conductors fail to make contact, the memory won't be recognized.

Okay, the memory's all seated properly and you know they're all the same. If you have any empty sockets, check the numbering of the sockets. Memory sockets need to be filled from Bank 0 (or 1, depending on how the sockets are numbered) on up. On some computers, if the initial bank is empty, the system won't see the memory that is installed. The computer will not boot. If the system uses Rambus memory, modules must be installed in pairs and all sockets must be filled, either with memory or with null devices called continuity modules.

If it's not a new computer, and you haven't performed any upgrades, you now ask, "What changed since the last time it worked?" Were any other components either added or replaced? As I mentioned before, it is possible for a stick of memory to get dislodged from its socket any time you're poking around inside the case.

Sometimes, however, the computer boots up just fine, but only a fraction of the memory is available to the user. On some computers, this is not an error. Motherboards with video adapters built in frequently grab a portion of system RAM to be used as video memory. This memory is reserved by the CMOS and is neither seen nor tested during POST. Only the memory left over after video RAM has been allocated will be reported. This doesn't qualify as a memory error. The system is doing its job correctly.

If a lack of memory is causing programs to not run, or making them run too slowly, go into the CMOS and allocate a smaller amount of memory for video. Some boards allow as much as 64MB (or more) of system memory to be used for video. On a computer that only has 64MB to start with, assigning 32MB for video probably isn't the wisest choice.

Once you've determined that the problem is really a problem, reread the first half of this Part. Everything I talked about concerning a computer that fails to boot due to memory errors also applies to computers that report memory incorrectly. However, there's another problem that might occur after an upgrade. If the first bank is recognized, the machine might recognize only that memory and continue the boot process. Memory installed in other sockets might go ignored. Therefore, check all the memory installed for poor seating or incorrect memory type.

It's easy to get spoiled by working only on computers that use nothing but DIMMs. One stick is always one bank. That's not the case with earlier Pentium-class machines that use SIMMs. You need two to fill a bank. If you try to get away with using just one, the machine will not boot at all. Also, trying to mix two sizes of memory in the same bank will halt the machine on boot up. In many cases, using two different speeds of memory in a bank will cause a boot failure. That's if you're lucky. Other times, the boot process is successful, but you end up with excessive numbers of memory errors while running applications.

Memory Errors in Applications

Much of the process of troubleshooting memory starts when the applications or operating system start reporting errors. Some of these are the result of situations I covered in the previous sections. Others are the result of how the application manages the memory it has available. Most of these errors can be resolved by restarting the system.

Some messages that suggest hardware failure overstate their case. Parity errors would suggest a bad memory module, yet frequently those errors are software related. The same holds true of General Protection Faults (GPF). I have seen so-called parity errors show up on machines using non-parity EDO.

"Out of Memory" errors don't always mean that you're actually out of memory. In Windows, that can simply mean that a particular application has used up the resources available to it. Another frequently seen message is "Stack Overflow." For the most part, these are errors gener-ated by the OS, not the hardware. As such, I don't want to go into a whole lot of detail as to what a stack overflow is or why it is bad. Any good book on operating systems can explain that. However, applica-tions installed by the user can generate some of these same errors. Even the best-designed application suffers from amnesia from time to time.

However, if the frequency of these error messages seems to be increas-ing, that's a good indication of hardware failure, either pending or imminent. Some good information hangs out in those error messages you've been roundly cursing. For example, in Windows, a fatal excep-tion error will report a memory address and a CPU register address where it thinks the fault occurred. Fatal exceptions occur when the CPU is asked to do the impossible, such as divide by zero, or when it is faced with an NMI it can't resolve. The address reported is usually right. If you've got a machine that is starting to come up with a lot of these messages, start keeping a log of those addresses. They're not as useless as they might look.

If the memory address is the same time and again, the next step is to find out what occupies that address. This isn't as impossible as it may sound. If the system is running Windows XP or NT, open up the Device Manager (get to it from the System icon in Control Panel). Make sure to set the View to Resources by Connection. There are two selections here that can help you find what memory addresses are in use by the system.

The first is Input/Output. All the I/O addresses in use are listed here. The address in the error message is in hexadecimal. Compare it to the ranges of addresses listed in Device Manager and see if the address reported by the error falls within any of these ranges. If so, you have found the piece of hardware causing the failure.

The other useful section is Memory. Some files, such as device drivers, load to the same address each time the system starts. Once again, you're reading in hex. Does your address show up here? If so, find out what that file relates to (if you can). If it is a device driver, reload the driver. If it is a system file, try getting a new copy of that file and copying over the one in your system. If the address does not appear, or the errors seem to occur randomly, it might be time to replace a memory module.

Windows 98 users can find all of this same information on their machines as well. To locate this data, go to Start>Settings>Control Panel, click on Systems, and select the main entry for the Computer. Click Properties, and there it is!

If you're got more than one memory module installed in your system, figuring out which one to replace can be a lot of fun. You can do it trial and error. Replace one and see if the problem goes away. If not, move on to the next one and try again. If you're a practicing professional, you'll probably want something a little more sophisticated. An application such as CheckIt Professional Edition by Touchstone Software or Ultra-X's Professional Diagnostics includes a utility for running diagnostics on the memory and locating the problem.

Memory errors don't always occur in main system memory. Add-on cards are frequently equipped with their own memory. Many of these devices use standard SIMM or DIMM modules. If that memory should fail, it will generate error messages just like the main system memory will. The best way to determine if this is the source of your problem is to start logging those errors all over again and try to determine if a particular piece of hardware is being accessed every time the error occurs.

Regardless of where the memory is located, memory does fail. The biggest reason any Integrated Circuit (IC) fails is electrostatic discharge. If a chip had to be handled at any time, for any reason, a spark might have killed it. Just remember, for you to even feel a spark of static electricity, that spark needs to be between 10,000 and 20,000 volts. Less than 2,000 volts can kill an IC. You can kill a memory chip or CPU and never even know it. If you actually feel a spark move from you to the chip, you can assume its dead, even if it appears to work at the outset.

Electrical surges in power can also damage memory. Too much current can destroy any circuit. And in fact, the memory can quite simply be getting old. You'd think that something with no moving parts would be immune to that. However, every substance in the world contains minute traces of radioactive elements, called isotopes. When a single molecule of an isotope decays, it will emit a burst of energy sufficient to destroy one or more of the individual memory cells in a RAM chip. This is going on every day of the chip's life. You don't miss one or two cells from a row or column in a single DRAM. But it's like your brain cells. When enough are gone, you can't remember if it's doing any harm or not. Unfortunately, it is.

I mentioned at the outset of this section that memory errors frequently mimicked those created by other devices. Every once in a while, the memory tests fine (you had it tested in a professional DIMM checker), applications errors are ruled out (you had Microsoft tech support on the phone for hours), and the errors are still occurring on a regular basis. It is now time for you to look at something besides memory for the source of the problem.

The CPU itself is a good source of memory-related issues. After all, it is the device that initiates virtually all memory I/O operations. Try to keep at least one or two current CPUs hanging around that you know to be good. Use a CPU you trust for a while and see if that makes the errors go away. If they do, the problem is solved.

If not, it's possible that the motherboard itself could be at fault. By now, it should be pretty clear that the chipset is arbitrating memory operations. If the chipset starts to fail, it can generate all kinds of eerie problems.

Memory problems are high on the list. A bad chipset can almost make you think the computer is haunted.

A problem that can drive you completely insane, and that you can never truly isolate, is when another chip, completely unrelated to memory begins to fail. Dying ICs can spill a lot of electronic noise out onto the circuit. This can be interpreted as random data, and can result in memory read errors.

In cases such as I've just described, a failing chipset or other IC, the only solution is to replace the system board. On most system boards, a failing CPU can be replaced.

Indecipherable Memory Errors

One of the things we've simply grown to accept about Windows is that it acts flaky from time to time. After a system has been running for a while, performance drops to a crawl. Perhaps functions in applications stop working the way they're supposed to. Maybe you can no longer cut and paste data from one location to another. Many of these errors are the result of how Windows "manages" memory. Win9x versions had some very notorious and well-documented memory leaks. When an application was opened, Windows would lock up a certain amount of physical RAM as well as a dedicated slice of virtual memory for that application to use. In theory, when the user closed out of that application, Windows would release all those resources for use by other applications.

Therein lies the difference between reality and theory. After a few hours of opening and closing applications, all of a sudden your machine with 256MB of SDRAM couldn't run WordPad without errors. The only solution was to restart the machine.

The next theory is that Win2K and WinXP plugged all of those memory leaks. Since I don't want to get into any arguments with Microsoft, suffice it to say that, even with these newer versions, if you are experiencing off-the-wall glitches, slugging performance, or erratic behavior, the best advice I can give you is REBOOT!

Memory For Other Uses

The PC isn't the only place where the computer geek uses memory. Your Pocket PC, your digital camera, and your PDA all need it, too. And how about transferring files back and forth between your office and home? There are a number of different memory technologies that need to be addressed here. These include micro drives and flash memory.

Flash Memory

Flash memory is the modern-day equivalent of the old EEPROM chips used by manufacturers to make BIOS chips. Flash can be classified as either NOR Flash or NAND Flash. These terms are derivative from the type of memory gate each one uses. NOR flash is typically slow and is used for firmware chips. NAND flash is much faster and sees a lot of use in memory cards. Generally, a product such as a digital camera will use both types. NOR flash will hold the camera's basic instruction set along with any user configuration data, while the digital film you purchased for holding your precious photos of Junior playing in the litter box is an example of NAND flash.

Another advantage of NAND flash for storing information such as digital images and other files is something called the Flash Translation Layer (FTL), developed in conjunction with the Personal Computer Memory Card International Association (PCMCIA) and M-Systems. This technology makes a flash card look and feel like a disk drive to most operating systems. NAND flash comes in a wide variety of packages:

✔ Type 1 and Type 2 ATA Flash Memory Cards (CompactFlash)
✔ SD Memory Cards
✔ SmartMedia
✔ MultiMediaCard
✔ Memory Stick

ATA Flash Memory

Originally developed by SanDisk, ATA flash memory is a very popular memory type among memory manufacturers. CompactFlash (**Figure 5.5**) is designed to work with either 3.3V or 5V devices. It sports a 50-pin interface, but easily slips into a 68-pin PCMCIA adapter card as long as that card fully complies with PCICIA specifications. These cards are both rugged and durable. They can withstand a drop from as high as ten feet without negative impact on the data stored within, don't require a constant power supply to retain their data, and are far less susceptible to corruption by external interference such as electromagnetic radiation. On top of that, they are very energy-efficient. A typical CompactFlash card consumes about 5 percent of the energy that a laptop hard disk eats up.

CompactFlash appears to the system the same way a hard disk does for one very simple reason. The memory card contains a single-chip ATA controller with all the embedded commands that any other IDE hard disk uses. Therefore, as far as the operating system is concerned, the CompactFlash card is a removable hard disk.

CompactFlash is available in Type I, Type II, and CF/IO formats. A Type I device measures 43mm (1.7″) × 36mm (1.4″) × 3.3mm (.13″). A Type II card has the same dimensions, except that it is 4.9mm (.19″) thick. A

Type I card can be used in a Type II slot. Obviously, however, it would take a really big hammer to get a Type II card to fit in a Type I slot. So don't even try it. CF/IO cards are not used for typical memory purposes, but rather for such devices as network cards, modems, and other devices.

Figure 5.5 An older 16MB CompactFlash card doesn't look any different than the 1GB card in my camera that recorded this image. In fact, in a pinch, I can use the 16MB card in my current camera to record **four whole pictures**!!

As far as data throughput, this varies widely with the product purchased. The original inventor of CompactFlash, SanDisk, sells four different types of CompactFlash card. **Table 5.4** lists these products, along with relative data throughputs and capacity ranges.

CompactFlash Product Table

Model	Data Throughput	Capacity Range
CompactFlash	1200KB-1600KB/sec	8MB to 512MB
Ultra II	9MB/sec	256MB to 8GB
Extreme	9MB/sec	256MB to 8GB
Extreme III	20MB/sec	256MB to 8GB

Table 5.4: The difference between the Ultra II and the Extreme is primarily the ability of the Extreme to withstand severe temperatures from −13° to 185°.

Secure Digital Memory Cards

Secure Digital (SD) memory cards are somewhat smaller than CompactFlash cards. They are 32mm × 24mm × 2.1mm in size. Another key difference between CompactFlash and SD is that the SD cards make use of a 9-pin connector. SD Memory is used when security is more of an issue. While the memory technology used is NAND flash, just like the CompactFlash, several enhancements make it a better choice when the information stored needs to be kept secure. Devices that use SD memory include digital music players, cellular telephones, and Global Positioning Systems (GPS) devices. Other improvements are targeted for information integrity. Overall, these enhancements include the following:

✔ Cryptographic security derived from technologies developed for DVD audio.

✔ The ability to enforce copyright protection.

✔ An improved casing that provides better protection from electrostatic discharge.

✔ A user-selectable mechanical write protect switch on the exterior card casing.

SmartMedia

SmartMedia, officially known as the Solid State Floppy Disk Card (SSFDC), is another form of NAND flash memory. Unlike the other types of flash memory I've discussed here, SmartMedia does not incorporate any controller circuitry of its own. It depends entirely upon the host system for a command set. At 47mm × 37mm × .76 mm, they are larger but thinner than some of the other cards I've discussed. SmartMedia cards operate at either 3.3V or 5V and incorporate a 22-pin interface. SmartMedia cards offer decent throughput at 8MB/s. However, since the largest ones available at the time of this writing are 128MB, they don't offer impressive capacity. SmartMedia cards see most of their use in the world of handheld computers and personal data assistants.

MultiMediaCard

A type of memory popular in cellular phones and ultra-tiny portable devices is the MultiMediaCard (MMC). MMCs are about the same size as SD memory at 32mm × 24mm × 1.4mm. They're about two-thirds thinner is all. They're designed to operate within a voltage range of 2.7 to 3.6V. Data throughput is only about 2.5MB/s.

Memory Stick

The advantage of MMC was its small size. The disadvantage is limited memory capacity. The Memory Stick is even smaller, at 31mm × 20mm × 1.6mm, and products are available with capacity of up to 512MB. These are fast devices as well, boasting data transfer rates of around 20MB/sec.

Figure 5.6

Memory sticks are probably the device that will be the death knell of the floppy diskette. This little device here fits on a keychain and holds the equivalent of just under 500 floppy disks worth of data. Now all the BIOS manufacturers need to do is make it a bootable device.

Part **6**

Graphics Adapters

A lot of articles talk about how much impact the graphics card has on system performance. In a way, that's actually not the case. A very fast video card won't make your CPU perform calculations any faster, nor will it make your game run faster. What it will do is make the graphics stream more smoothly across the screen, with fewer jitters and less commotion. So as far as the user is concerned, the system is running faster. Video cards are one of the more difficult components for a user to choose and offer some of the most unusual options. I'll start with choosing a video card, and then move on to installation and troubleshooting.

Choosing a Video Card

There are several things that you need to consider when purchasing a new video card. Some have to do with raw speed, while others have to do with software compatibility. Things to consider include the following:

✔ Graphics subsystem interface
✔ Video chipset
✔ Graphics processor
✔ RAMDAC
✔ Video memory
✔ API support

While any one of these factors considered separately can have anywhere from negligible to slight impact on overall performance, a solid combination of all factors working on all cylinders can result in a dramatic performance increase. The key is in making sure that you're buying the right card for the purpose at hand.

For more information on The Mechanics of Graphics Adapters, go to page 388, Chapter 16 of *The Complete Guide to A+ Certification*.

The Graphics Subsystem Interface

At this point in time there are really only two interfaces to discuss: AGP and PCI-X. AGP has been around for a while, and is a tried and true interface with several available options. PCI-X is the new kid on the block with blazing speed, questionable compatibility, and a high price. But if you know for certain it's going to work for you, and if your pockets are deep enough, it's definitely the way to go.

AGP

The Accelerated Graphics Port (AGP) was designed exclusively with graphics in mind, which is probably why its called a graphics port. A system can only use one AGP device at a time. There cannot be two AGP devices. All AGP devices run at a 66MHz clock speed. The original AGP devices could transmit one bit on each clock cycle. AGP 2x transfers two bits of data per clock cycle, AGP 4x bumps it up to four bits, and coincidentally enough, 8x AGP manages 8 bits per clock cycle.

A couple of things to consider before sinking loads of cash into an 8x card. The first is performance. Most independent reviews that I read didn't show much of an improvement in speed when jumping from 4x to 8x. In fact, there was hardly any increase at all. Much of the reason for that lies in the applications programming. Second, the 8x cards, for the most part, all required more extensive cooling requirements and not all applications supported them anyway.

That doesn't mean an application that doesn't support 8x can't be used if you install an 8x card. An AGP 2x card has no problem running in an AGP 8x slot and vice versa. But the card will never run faster than its maximum capability. It can, however, be forced to run slower than its peak. If the CMOS setup is configured for 2x and you have a 4x card installed, you're losing half the potential speed of your card.

AGP Pro is not a faster interface, but rather a higher-powered one. Fast video processors and lots of fast memory on a video card call for a lot of power to make it work. A standard AGP slot is designed to provide 25W of power. This isn't enough for many of the new high-end adapters. AGP-PRO50 ups the ante to 50W, while AGP-PRO110 delivers more power than a 100-watt light bulb. Now, remember how hot that 100W light bulb gets? That's how hot that video card can get as well. That's why there is such a humungous fan on one of these video cards. The size of the fan forces you to lose a slot.

PCI-X

PCI Express, or PCI-X as it is more commonly known, doesn't look to be all that much faster at a casual glance. It starts out with a 133MHz bus. Okay, that's twice as fast as the raw clock speed of AGP. However, two things combine to push PCI-X far beyond AGP's envelope. One of these is that the bus can already work at 16x. Second, it can work at 16x in a bidirectional communications mode. The end result is a bus that clocks up to 8GB/s in bandwidth, compared to the 2GB maximum of AGP 8x. In theory, this should lead to almost lifelike displays of extremely high-speed action. In reality, we just don't know yet. It's too new and programmers aren't writing specifically to the interface. So actual performance at this point in time is about the same as AGP. But the potential is certainly there.

The Video Chipset

This isn't anything you have control over. When you select the make and model of a video card, you select the chipset. However, the chipset controls two critical functions. One is the type and amount of video memory that is supported. This will be discussed when I talk about frame buffers. The other thing it controls is the set of Application Programming Interfaces (APIs) that it supports. An API is a collection of programming code that all applications use to communicate with a specific device. Many programs, most notably computer games, are quite specific as to the graphical APIs they support.

The Graphics Processor

Unlike computer motherboards, video cards don't have a single CPU. Graphics cards feature multiple chips performing specialized functions. One of these is the graphics processor. The graphics processor is the chip that intercepts the commands issued by the video card device driver and executes them.

Operations performed by the graphics processor are the functions that created a digitized image using polygons, circles, and squares. Once the graphics processor has drawn a frame, it dumps that information into the frame buffer. These functions would include changing window sizes in your OS, rendering different font sizes, and following the grenade from your RPG to the monster attacking Tokyo. For gamers, high speed is a must.

Video Memory

The frame buffer is nothing more than a memory pool where information is stored until it's ready to be used. The type of video memory used in the manufacture of your video card impacts graphics performance. The amount of memory dictates how many textures can be rendered and stored in the buffer until needed. Over the years, there have been a variety of memory types used on video cards. These days, the choice has boiled down to DDR and DDR2.

Table 5.1 lists some of the different types of memory used and the usage each type saw.

> For more information on How Memory Works, go to page 174, Chapter 9 of *The Complete Guide to A+ Certification.*

Memory used in Graphics Adapters

Type	Description	Relative Speed	Relative Cost	Relative Usage
FPM	Fast Page Mode	Very Slow	N/A	Obsolete
EDO	Extended Data Out	Slow	Cheap	Low-end and OEM
SGRAM	Synchronized Graphics RAM	Moderate	Cheap	Mid-range and OEM
WRAM	Windows RAM	Fast	N/A	Obsolete
VRAM	Video RAM	Fast	Fairly expensive	Now obsolete
DDR	Double Data Rate RAM	Extremely fast	Moderate	High-end cards
DDR2	The newest version of DDR	The fastest available	Expensive	High-end cards
MDRAM	Multibank DRAM	Extremely fast	Extremely expensive	Rarely used

Table 5.1: It is not unheard of for some high-end video cards to make use of two different types of memory on one card. Fast memory will be used for functions related to video processing, while a slower type might be used for storing texture maps.

Video memory comes into play during two stages of the development of a single screen you see on your monitor. The first time it is used is to store the texture maps programmers use in creating their images. If each texture on a complex graphic had to be redrawn from scratch on each and every screen that was being drawn at, say 80Hz, performance would be slow even with today's technology. Instead, only the outlines of images are drawn for each screen, and the textures are filled in from maps that are already stored in memory. The more memory a video card has the more texture maps that can be stored.

Memory comes into play a second time after the RAMDAC, discussed in the next section, has assembled a screen. While one screen is being displayed on the monitor, the next one is stored in memory. This prevents any delays. It is this storage that results in the term frame buffer.

The RAMDAC

The Random Access Memory Digital Analog Converter (RAMDAC) is another chip that directly affects video card performance by its speed. Like a CPU, the RAMDAC is rated for speed in megahertz. It is the chip that takes digital information from the frame buffer and converts it to an RGB signal. Since streaming video and game animation both depend heavily on how many frames your video card can produce in a second, this is a key feature to look at. It isn't uncommon these days for a high-end graphics adapter to feature two matched RAMDACs.

API Support

All video cards will work as standard video cards, regardless of settings. But to perform some of their more advanced magical tricks, such as high-speed 3-D rendering, they depend on different APIs. There are a few generic APIs that nearly all video cards support. Then, in the spirit of competition, a few of the more advanced APIs are specific to certain brands. Some applications, specifically games, require certain APIs to be loaded in order to run properly. When shopping for a video card, consider all the applications you intend to run and figure out which card is best suited for your repertoire.

Installing Video Cards

For the most part, installing video cards is a no-brainer. You seat the card into the proper slot, fire up the machine and let Plug 'n Play do its thing. Because most operating systems won't have drivers for the newest adapters in their databases, most of the time, you will need to provide a diskette or CD with the drivers. The complete installation process is described in the next two sections.

Installing the Hardware

1. Open the computer's enclosure.
2. If you are replacing an existing video card, remove the old one and store it in an antistatic bag, unless it's dead. If it's dead it doesn't matter how careful you are.

3. Seat the new video card in the slot, making sure it is properly seated, both front and rear. Most AGP slots have a snap that holds the card in place.

4. Close the case and hook the computer back up. When you fire it up for the first time after installation, one of two things is going to happen (assuming that the video card you removed was your original problem).

   - The computer will boot properly, and you go onto the next step.
   - The computer will issue a series of beeps and refuse to boot. Go to the troubleshooting procedures section at the end of this Part.

5. On the first boot, most new video cards will not be recognized by the OS as anything but a standard VGA adapter. Resolution will be limited to 640×480 and you will only have 16 colors. *Usually* on reboot, your OS tells you that new hardware was detected and leads you through a driver installation routine.

Installing the Drivers

If the OS fails to realize that it needs to install new drivers, you'll need to surgically implant them. This was a fairly common problem with Win9x and an occasional problem with Win2K, but it rarely happens with WinXP. I'm not going to go through each and every version of Windows in showing you how to install the drivers. The methods just don't vary that much. The following procedures are based on Win2K

1. Go to Start>Settings>Control Panel. Scroll down and double-click the System icon.

2. Click the Hardware tab, then click Device Manager. In Device Manager, click the + sign next to Display Adapters.

3. Right-click your adapter and select Properties. Click the Driver tab, and in the following screen, click the Update Drivers button. This starts the Update Drivers Wizard.

4. Follow the path of the Wizard, accepting all defaults, with this exception. When it asks you to search for a driver, make sure that in the Locate Driver Files window only the drive that contains your drivers is checked.

5. Once the installation is complete, even if Windows doesn't prompt you to restart your computer, restart anyway. After that, you can configure your display adapter however you please.

The Digital Video Interface

Since today's VGA adapters do not fully support the use of digital monitors, a new standard was needed. The Digital Display Working Group designed the Digital Video Interface (DVI) for this purpose. Because VGA technology requires that the signal be converted from digital to analog for transmission to the monitor, a certain amount of degradation occurs. DVI keeps data in digital form from the computer to the monitor, virtually eliminating signal loss. The DVI specification is based on Silicon Image's Transition Minimized Differential Signaling (TMDS) and provides a high-speed digital interface. TMDS takes the signal from the graphics adapter, determines the resolution and refresh rate that the monitor is using, and spreads the signal out over the available bandwidth to optimize the data transfer from computer to monitor. DVI is technology-independent. Essentially, this means that DVI is going to perform properly with any display and graphics card that is DVI compliant. If you buy a DVI monitor, make sure that you have a video adapter card that can connect to it.

There are three basic DVI formats, and a fourth, less common one, that you might run into. DVI-D is pure digital. For this you require a DVI interface on both the display adapter and on the monitor. DVI-A produces an analog signal. It doesn't provide quite the quality of DVI-D, but its quality is noticeably better than standard VGA. DVI-I provides both a digital and an analog interface. The DVI interface that isn't as common is the P&D interface. It, like DVI-I, provides both digital and analog signals.

It sounds like it should be simple, right? However, the different levels of DVI support have resulted in several different types of connectors (as opposed to the single type of VGA connector). Only six are commonly seen. These are described in the next few paragraphs.

DVI-D

DVI-D is available in single-link and dual-link configurations. The difference between the two is that dual-link DVI provides two separate TMDS channels for better resolution, definition, and color gamut. Very high-end LCD monitors, such as Apple's Cinema displays and plasma screens, will require dual-link support. Most conventional LCD screens don't require dual-link connections, but will still benefit greatly. Better LCD displays provide dual-link support. **Figure 6.1** and **Figure 6.2** illustrate DVI-D single-link and DVI-D dual-link connections.

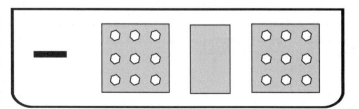

Figure 6.1 A DVI-D single-link connector

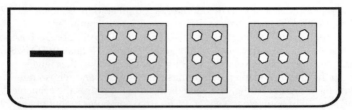

Figure 6.2   A DVI-D dual-link connector

DVI-A and P&D Connectors

DVI-A also comes in two different incarnations. Straight analog connectors are strictly for sending a signal out to analog monitors. The P&D connector provides both digital and analog signals and is occasionally found on PC-based graphics adapters and specialty cards. **Figure 6.3** and **Figure 6.4** show the DVI connectors that support analog signals.

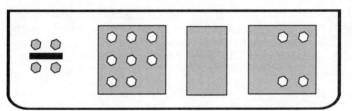

Figure 6.3   An analog-only DVI-A connector

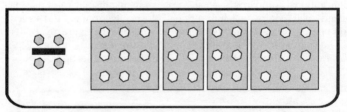

Figure 6.4   A hybrid DVI connector that supports both digital and analog signals

DVI-I

As with the DVI-D connectors, DVI-I is also available in single- and dual-link configurations. The reasoning is the same. DVI-I connectors are shown below in **Figure 6.5** and **Figure 6.6**.

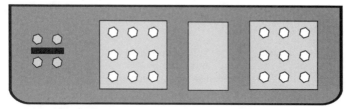

Figure 6.5   A DVI-I single-link connector

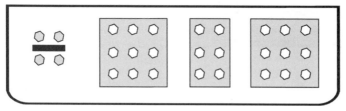

Figure 6.6   A DVI-I single-link connector

Troubleshooting Video Cards

When your video card doesn't work, the problem is generally going to fall into one of three categories. The card itself is bad; there is a hardware conflict preventing it from being recognized; or driver issues prevent it from working properly. Hardware problems are generally fixed on the BIOS level. A fourth type of problem occurs when the video card is working, but it just isn't working the way you want it to. Those issues will be discussed separately.

The Card is Bad

You've been using your computer for some time and suddenly it won't boot any more. When you start your machine, it issues a series of beeps and then shuts down. If you get the same series of beeps even after removing the video card and attempting to start the machine without a video card, that is usually a sign of a failed video card. The easiest way to test this is to install a known-good adapter and try to boot the system again. If the system boots, problem solved. If it doesn't, then perhaps the problem isn't with the video card, but rather with the motherboard. Run a hardware diagnostics utility.

Hardware Conflicts

If there is a hardware conflict, you'll know right away. The computer will give out a series of beeps and instantly lock up. Remove the video card and you will hear the same series of beeps.

The most common cause of a new video card not working immediately after installation is that the BIOS configuration needs to be tweaked. Many motherboards offer both onboard video as well as an AGP port. Since the onboard video is likely to be AGP-based as well, you have to remember that only one AGP device can exist on the system at once. There will be some place in your CMOS setup where you can go to disable onboard graphics and tell your machine to boot to the AGP slot. Most often, this is located in the Chipset Features portion of BIOS. Some brands have an Onboard Peripherals section where you will find this setting.

> For more information on The Programs of ROM BIOS, go to page 118 Chapter 6 of *The Complete Guide to A+ Certification.*

Driver Conflicts

Driver conflicts rarely cause your system to fail to start. The system boots fine, but all you get is 640×480 resolution with 16 colors. The resolution to this problem is described in the section Installing Video Cards.

General Troubleshooting

If you're having trouble with a video card, chances are extremely good that you're having a driver-related issue or are having an argument with your OS (you'll never win, by the way). If the graphics card is letting you see the screen, it is most likely doing its job. There are some little quirks here and there that are related to the video card. Some can be easily fixed, and others can be easily fixed by replacing the video card.

✔ **The system goes through the whole boot process (or seems to) without ever once giving me a screen, but I don't get any beeps.** Check your cable. It helps to have the monitor hooked up to the computer.

✔ **I get a long series of short beeps (usually eight) and the boot process stops.** You have an AMI BIOS and a video card failure. Try a new one. If you have an Award BIOS, this could mean bad memory instead.

✔ **I get one long beep and two short beeps and the boot process stops.** You have an Award BIOS. See above.

✔ **The computer boots fine, but all I can ever get is standard VGA.** This is a driver issue. Reload the drivers and try again. And this time try loading the correct drivers.

✔ **The computer boots fine until Windows starts to load and then the screen goes blank.** See above.

✔ **Windows loads fine, and I can select all the settings I want, but I keep getting sparkly little crystals all over the place, or black specks everywhere.** This is usually caused by bad video memory. If your card has replaceable memory, swap it out. Since video cards these days usually have it soldered on, it's a good excuse to get that new 256MB X-Force Accelerator Card you've been begging your significant other for.

✔ **My picture is a lovely shade of puke green/fuchsia/magenta/olive drab/cyan/whatever.** Check the pins on the monitor cable. One of them is probably bent. And then stop blaming the video card. It has nothing to do with it.

Part 7

Operating Systems Issues

The remainder of the book will deal with operating system (OS) issues and a short section on networking computers. Rather than get into specific discussions about brands of OS, I'll avoid general discussion and simply provide some tips; lists of Windows hotkeys, general error messages you'll encounter, and commonly used ports; and some assistance in interpreting the famed blue screen of death.

Windows Functions

While Windows was designed to be a point-and-click graphical interface that relies heavily on the mouse, many users find that the mouse is more cumbersome than the keyboard for many simple tasks. Microsoft realized this and provided quite a large number of keyboard shortcuts.

For more information on Making Your Way Around Windows, go to page 596, Chapter 24 of *The Complete Guide to A+ Certification*.

I'm sure that the astute reader will be able to point out a number of shortcuts that I've missed, but **Table 7.1** provides some of the most commonly used (and convenient) ones. Hope it helps speed up your work!

Windows Hotkey Shortcuts

Shortcut	Action
<Alt>	Activates or deactivates the current window's menu bar.
<Delete>	Delete selected item(s).
Drag 'n Drop	Select an object or objects. Press and hold left mouse button. Drag selected object(s) over to the icon that depicts the desired destination folder or device and then release. This generally moves the selected object from its original place to the new one.
Right-click Drag 'n Drop	Does the same as drag 'n drop (above) but also brings up a pop-up menu that offers a number of different options. The options offered depend on the object being moved, and the target location.
<End>	Moves cursor to end of current line, except for Internet Explorer. In IE, it's moved to the bottom of the page.
<Enter>	Opens selected item or activates highlighted button.
<Esc>	Cancels current operation.
<F1>	Displays context-sensitive help for selected item.
<F2>	In Explorer, activates the Rename command.
<F3>	In Explorer, opens a file search.
<F4>	In Explorer, displays My Computer menu. In IE, displays Address History list.
<F5>	Refreshes the contents of the current window.
<F6>	Switches between active panes of current application.
<Home>	Moves cursor to beginning of line (except IE). In IE moves to the top of the page.
Menu Button	Duplicates the function of the right mouse button.
<Print Screen>	Copies the current screen to clipboard as bitmap image.
Space Bar	Toggles current checkbox or radio button.
<Tab>	Moves between fields and/or objects of current window.
Windows Button	Opens the Start menu.

<Ctrl> Shortcuts

Shortcut	Action
<Ctrl>+A	Selects all items.
<Ctrl>+<Alt>+	Win98: Opens Close Programs window. Win2K or XP:

Shortcut	Action
<Delete>	Open Security window (allows you to lock workstation, log off, shutdown, change password, and start Task Manager)
<Ctrl>+ <Backspace>	Deletes all text from the cursor to beginning of current word or punctuation mark.
<Ctrl>+C	Copies the selected item(s) to the Windows Clipboard.
<Ctrl>+Drag 'n Drop	Copies selected file(s) or directory(s) to target location.
<Ctrl>+<Esc>	Opens the Windows Start menu.
<Ctrl>+F	Opens a text search for current window.
<Ctrl>+<F4>	Closes active window.
<Ctrl>+G	Go To function. Allows user to move to a selected page in document.
<Ctrl>+H	In Office applications, opens a Search and Replace. In IE, it opens a History bar.
<Ctrl>+<Home>	Moves cursor to beginning of document.
<Ctrl>+<End>	Moves cursor to end of document.
<Ctrl>+<Insert>	Copies selected item(s) to Windows Clipboard.
<Ctrl>+Left Arrow	Moves cursor to previous word in the document.
<Ctrl>+N	Opens a new file or window.
<Ctrl>+O	Starts the File>Open function.
<Ctrl>+P	Prints the contents of the current window.
<Ctrl>+Right Arrow	Moves cursor to the next word in the document.
<Ctrl>+S	Saves the current file to previous location on disk.
<Ctrl>+<Shift> +<Esc>	In Win98, opens the Start menu. In Win2K or XP, opens Task Manager.
<Ctrl>+V	Pastes the contents of Windows Clipboard to selected location.
<Ctrl>+X	Cuts the selected item(s) from its current location and copies it to the Windows Clipboard.
<Ctrl>+Y	Repeats the previous action.
<Ctrl>+Z	Reverses the previous action.

<Alt> Shortcuts

Shortcut	Action
<Alt>+ <Backspace>	Reverses the previous action (similar to <Ctrl>+Z).
<Alt>+ Double-click	In a document, selects entire document.
<Alt>+<Enter>	Repeats previous action.
<Alt>+<F4>	Closes the current window.

continues

<Alt> Shortcuts (*continued*)

Shortcut	Action
<Alt>+<Print Screen>	Copies current window to Windows Clipboard as bitmap image.
<Alt>+Space Bar	Open current Window's controls (Restore, Move, Size, Minimize, Maximize, Close).
<Alt>+<Tab>	Switches between active Applications (while holding <Alt>, hit <Tab> or <Shift>+<Tab> to go to next or previous app; release <Alt> to restore the selected app).

<Shift> Shortcuts

Shortcut	Action
<Shift>+<Alt>+<Tab>	Switch among running applications (while holding <Alt>, hit <Tab> or <Shift>+<Tab> to go to next or previous app; release <Alt> to restore the selected app).
<Shift>+<Delete>	In Windows Explorer, deletes selected item(s) immediately and does not move them to the Recycle Bin. In other apps, selected items are cut and moved to Windows Clipboard.
<Shift>+Down Arrow	Selects all of current line. Repeating the function selects the next line.
<Shift>+Drag 'n Drop selected file(s)	Move File(s) to target folder except when target folder is Recycle Bin. When moving to Recycle Bin, it deletes the file(s) permanently.
<Shift>+<Insert>	Pastes the contents of Windows Clipboard to selected location.
<Shift>+Left Arrow	Removes the previous character from text selection.
<Shift>+<Print Screen>	Copies current window to clipboard as bitmap image.
<Shift>+Right Arrow	Adds the current character to selected text.
<Shift>+<Tab>	Moves to previous field or control in current window.
<Shift>+Up Arrow	Removes previous line from selected text.

Windows Key Shortcuts

Shortcut	Action
[⊞]+<Ctrl>+F	Allows user to search for a specific computer on the network.
[⊞]+D	Minimizes (or restores when repeated) all open windows (does not work in Win95).
[⊞]+E	Launches Windows Explorer, starting with My Computer.

Shortcut	Action
+F	Opens a Find Files window.
+<F1>	Launches Windows Help.
+L	Locks the computer when connected to a network domain, or switches users on a computer not connected to a network domain (WinXP only).
+M	Minimizes current window.
+<Pause /Break>	Opens the Control Panel System Properties applet.
+G	Quick-switches between users (WinXP only).
+R	Opens a Run dialog box in the Start menu.
+<Shift>+M	Restores all minimized windows.
+<Tab>	Cycles through the buttons on the Task Bar.
+U	Launches the Accessibility Utility Manager (WinXP only).
+V	Open Voice Settings (Narrator Settings window must be open) (Win2K/XP only).

Table 7.1: Windows and Windows applications contain a large number of keyboard shortcuts called hotkeys.

Commonly Used Ports

Ports are doorways to the operating system from the outside. When hooked up to the Internet or some other exposure to the outside world, it is important to close any doors that aren't being used. To do so, you can install a piece of software known as a firewall onto your system. Properly configuring a firewall requires that you know precisely what ports you need and which ones are safe to close. **Table 7.2** lists some commonly used ports.

Commonly Used Ports

Port	Description / Use
7	Echo (used by PING)
15	Netstat
20	File Transfer Protocol (data)
21	FTP (control)

continues

Commonly Used Ports (*continued*)

Port	Description / Use
22	Secure Telnet / SSH
25	Simple Mail Transfer Protocol
42	Nameserve and WINS
53	Domain Name Services
67	BOOTP
68	BOOTP/DHCP
69	Trivial File Transfer Protocol
79	Finger
80	Hypertext Transport Protocol
88	Kerberos
98	LINUXCONF
109	Post Office Protocol, Version 2
110	Post Office Protocol, Version 3
115	Simple File Transfer Protocol
119	Network News
123	Network Time
139	NetBIOS
143	Internet Message Access Protocol, Version 2
161	Simple Network Management Protocol
194	Internet Relay Chat
220	Internet Message Access Protocol, Version 3
387	AppleTalk Update-based Routing Protocol
389	Lightweight Directory Access Protocol
443	Secure Socket Layer
444	Simple Network Paging Protocol
520	Routing Information Protocol
540	Unix-to-Unix Copy Protocol
666	Network DOOM (You GOTTA know that one!!)

Table 7.2: If you are using a protocol regularly, keep the port open on your firewall. If not, close it down.

Common Socket Errors

Sockets are similar to ports, except that they communicate directly to applications. As such, they can be a bit more difficult to troubleshoot. **Table 7.3** lists some common socket errors you might see.

Socket Errors and Their Descriptions

Error Number	Description
10004	Interrupted function call
10013	Permission denied
10014	Invalid address
10022	Invalid argument
10024	Too many open files
10035	Resource temporarily unavailable
10036	Operation currently in progress
10037	This operation already in progress
10038	Attempted operation on non-socket
10039	Destination address required
10040	Excessive message length
10041	Incorrect protocol for socket
10042	Invalid protocol option
10043	Protocol not supported
10044	Socket type not supported
10045	Operation not supported
10046	Protocol family not supported
10047	Address family not supported by protocol family
10048	Address already in use
10049	Cannot assign requested address
10050	Network unavailable
10051	Network unreachable
10052	Network lost connection during reset
10053	Connection aborted by software call
10054	Connection reset by peer
10055	Buffer overflow
10056	Socket already connected
10057	Socket not connected
10058	Cannot send after socket shutdown
10060	Connection timed out
10061	Connection refused
10064	Host is down
10065	No route to host
10067	Too many processes
10091	Network subsystem is unavailable
10092	WINSOCK.DLL version out of range
10093	Successful WSAStartup not yet performed
10094	Graceful shutdown in progress
11001	Host not found

continues

Socket Errors and Their Descriptions (*continued*)

Error Number	Description
11002	Non-authoritative host not found
11003	Non-recoverable error
11004	Valid name, Invalid data type requested

Table 7.3: Socket errors aren't as common as they used to be, but they still occasionally raise their ugly heads.

Problems with Windows Startup

One of the things that can make a computer system take forever and a day to start up first thing in the morning has absolutely nothing to do with whether or not it's had its coffee. It seems that every little application or device you ever install assumes that you want to have access to it twenty-four hours a day, seven days a week. So it puts itself into your Startup menu. After a while, you end up with so many applications launching automatically at startup that you have time for breakfast and the morning paper while you're waiting for your system to boot.

Win9x and WinXP have a utility called MSCONFIG that allows you to easily configure your startup options. Win2K, for some reason, saw fit to leave this utility out. However, the WinXP version works fine in Win2K and as of this writing can be downloaded off of Microsoft's Downloads site. To start MSCONFIG, click Start>Run and type MSCONFIG into the command line. **Table 7.4** lists the entries that you might find cluttering up your system. Some are actually viruses and it is critical that you not only remove the entry from startup, but run a good antivirus program to get rid of the malware as well.

For more information on MSCONFIG, go to page 628, Chapter 24 of *The Complete Guide to A+ Certification*.

Annotated List of MSCONFIG Startup Entries

Program or File Name	Description
(Default)=%SysDir%\matcher.exe	Virus removal instructions for the virus W32/Matcher@MM
1on1mail.htm	Virus removal instructions for the virus VBS.1ON1MAIL
3com Modem Manager or MDMMGR.EXE	Status icon for 3Com modems
3dfx Task Manager	Configuration applet for Voodoo video cards
3dfx Tools	Tools applet for Voodoo video cards

Program or File Name	Description
3Dqtl.exe	A function of Terratec128i PCI sound card drivers. This loads a sound profile at boot up, restoring volume and other audio settings to a predetermined default. (Not mandatory)
A1000 Settings Utility or CPQA1000.EXE	Compaq A1000 Print Fax All-in-One copy scan printer software. Required in Startup in order to scan, print, copy, and fax.
Access Ramp Monitor or ARMON32.EXE	A program that monitors the status of an Internet connection. (Not mandatory)
Acrobat Assistant or ACROTRAY.EXE or [ACROTRAY]	An Acrobat Reader function that converts Postscript documents to PDF. (Not mandatory)
Active CPU or ACPU.EXE or [ACTIVE CPU]	Generates a graphical representation of CPU activity. (Not mandatory)
Adaptec DirectCD or DIRECTCD.EXE	Allows a formatted CD-RW or CD-R disc to have files written directly to it from Explorer.
Adaware Bootup or AD-AWARE.EXE or [AD-AWARE 5]	Spyware removal utility. (Not mandatory)
Adobe Gamma Loader	Calibrates monitor colors more closely to print colors for Adobe applications. (Not mandatory)
AGSatellite (AGSatellite.exe)	A function of AudioGalaxy software that lets you download MP3 files from their server. (Not mandatory)
AHQTB	Audio Headquarters for a Creative Labs SoundBlaster Live! sound card. (Not mandatory)
AIM Reminder	A function of AOL's Instant Messenger service. (Not mandatory)
AIM Reminder.exe	A virus that mimics the real AIM Reminder.
Alexa	Function of Alexa Toolbar 5.0. An Internet Navigation tool that provides information about the site being viewed. (Not mandatory)
ALOGSERV.EXE	Function of McAfee Antivirus. Logs scanning activities. (Not mandatory, and has been known to cause issues with some programs)
AMD POWERNOW! or GEMBACK.EXE	AMD PowerNow! utility. Maximizes battery life by decreasing CPU speed when the system is running on battery power. Required on some laptops.
Anti or anti.exe or [anti]	Automatically clicks AOL's idle/timer popup windows, preventing the user from being forcibly signed off.
anvshell or ANVSHELL.EXE	Puts display properties settings onto an icon in the system tray. (Not mandatory)
AOL Instant Messenger or AIM.EXE	AOL Instant Messenger. (Not mandatory)
AOLTRAY.EXE	Puts AOL icon in system tray. (Not mandatory)

continues

Annotated List of MSCONFIG Startup Entries (*continued*)

Program or File Name	Description
ARMON32.EXE	Monitor an Internet connection for hang-ups, connection speeds, internet congestion, and traffic flow. (Not mandatory)
Astro or ATRO.EXE	A utility included with Quicken personal finance software. (Not mandatory)
ASUS Tweak Enable or ASTART.EXE	A utility that is placed on the system tray when the settings for certain ASUS graphics adapters have been configured beyond their normal settings. Allows other changes and/or restoring factory default settings. (Not mandatory)
ATI GART Setup Utility	Checks the motherboard chipset and determines which drivers to install for certain ATI cards. Once the drivers are installed, it should be removed.
ATI Scheduler	Function of ATI driver that remains RAM resident and automatically launches the ATI video player at time and date pre-selected by the user. Remove if not being used.
ATI Task Application	Launches display settings for ATI graphics cards. (Not mandatory)
ATI*.* (various different files)	These are associated with an ATI Rage graphics card. (Not mandatory)
AtiCwd32 or ATICWD32.EXE	ATI graphics card system tray. (Not mandatory, but useful)
ATIKEY or ATITASK.EXE or [atitask]	Shortcut to various programs, display settings, and the ATI Desktop online help system. Should not be kept in startup, but rather run from Start menu when needed.
Attune Download	Monitors PC hardware and provides a shortcut to a PC help network. Use with caution.
AttuneClientEngine or ATTUNE_CE.EXE	Provides a notification service for Attune. (Not mandatory)
AudioHQ	Desktop control panel for the Creative Labs Live! card. (Not mandatory)
Aureal 3D Interactive Audio (a3dinit.exe)	3D positional sound controls for Compaq PC's with Aureal-based 3D soundcards. If removed, only standard sound can be obtained.
AutoEA or AHQRUN.EXE	A function of Creative Labs Soundblaster Live! series soundcards. Allows user to specify what audio preset to automatically associate for any audio application. (Not mandatory)
AutoUpdate or XUPDATE.EXE	Function of McAfee Antivirus that verifies that the software is up to date. (Not mandatory. Can update manually.)

Program or File Name	Description
AV Console or AVCONSOL.EXE or [avconsol]	Function of McAfee Antivirus that scans local or network drives automatically on a user-defined schedule. (Not mandatory)
BACKWEB or USERPROF.EXE	A Compaq service that automatically detects internet connection and downloads any available updates. (Not mandatory)
Battery Bar	Laptop utility that estimates remaining battery power. (Not mandatory, but useful)
BayMgr	Dell laptop utility that allows swapping a battery, DVD, or other item in an accessory bay.
BCDetect or BCDETECT.EXE	A function of Creative Labs that detects when the correct drivers are installed for the video card. It loads the BlasterControl when the drivers are detected. (Not mandatory)
BCMDMMSG or BCMDMMSG.EXE	The modem messaging applet for BCM V.90 56k modems. Required for dial-up if you have one of these modems.
BCMHal or BCMHAL9X.DLL or [bcinit]	Places Display properties for Creative Labs graphics adapters onto system tray. (Not mandatory)
BCTweak or BCTWEAK.EXE	A utility that allows the user to adjust certain settings on Creative Labs graphics adapters. (Not mandatory)
BillMinder or REMIND32	A function of Quicken that reminds the user of due payments. (Not mandatory)
BitMagic or BITLOADER.EXE	A function of Bitmagic's Bitplayer that places the menu options into the toolbar. (Not mandatory)
BlackICE utility or BLACKICE.EXE	A function of Network ICE firewall that places certain menu options on the toolbar. Closing it will close the firewall. No point in removing it. It will reappear on next reboot unless you edit the registry.
BLSTAPP or BLSTAPP.EXE	Puts access to Creative's BlasterControl in the system tray. (Not mandatory)
bmlic-1 or LOADER.EXE	A function of Bitmagic's Bitplayer that places certain menu items in the toolbar. Also checks for updates when Internet connection is present. (Not mandatory)
Bonzai Buddy	Talking parrot and monkey. A form of spyware. Run a spyware removal utility to get rid of it.
BMO MasterCard Wallet or EWALLET.EXE	Stores your credit card and other personal information in an encrypted file on your PC so that any talented hacker can access it. (Not mandatory)
bombshel or BOMB32.EXE	A function of McAfee Nuts & Bolts. Protects your Windows system from application failure and crashes. (Not mandatory)
BPCPOST or BPCPOST.EXE	Post-setup program for Microsoft TV Viewer. Can be removed after installation is complete.

continues

Annotated List of MSCONFIG Startup Entries (*continued*)

Program or File Name	Description
Cal reminder shortcut	Manages the pop-ups used by MS Works Calendar as reminders. (Not mandatory)
CallControl or FTCTRL32.EXE	A function of FaxTalk Messenger Pro that allows any TAPI-compliant application to access the modem from Windows. (Not mandatory)
Cardscan 300start or CSRESET.EXE	A function of the Cardscan 300 scanner driver that resets the scanner on startup. (Not mandatory)
CBWAttn or CBWATTN.EXE or CBWHost or CBWHOST.EXE	A function of Bitware fax software that answers incoming faxes. Not required for outgoing faxes and has known issues with Windows Power Management.
CC2KUI or COMET.EXE	A program that allows the user to change cursors on the fly. (Not mandatory)
CIJ3P2PSERVER or CIJ3P2PS.EXE	Compaq printer utility. Required for the printer work correctly.
CISRVR Program or CISRVR.EXE	Compaq Internet setup wizard. (Not mandatory)
CleanSweep or Smart Sweep or Internet Sweep	Function of Norton CleanSweep. Can be started manually. (Not mandatory)
ClickTheButton or CTB.EXE	A function of Bonzai Buddy, a form of spyware. Run a spyware removal utility to get rid of it.
ClipMate5x or CLIPMT5X.EXE	A utility that allows the user to maintain multiple items in the Windows Clipboard. (Not mandatory, but can be useful)
Colorific Control Panel (Hgcctl95.exe)	A color-matching utility from E_Color. Assures accurate gamma and color temperature between your monitor and other still imaging devices. (Not mandatory, but may be useful)
Compaq C3-1000 Settings Utility or cpqc31k.exe or [cpqc31k.exe]	Compaq printer utility. Required in order for the printer to work.
Compaq Internet Setup or INETWIZARD.EXE	Compaq Internet setup wizard. (Not mandatory)
Compaq Knowledge Center or SILENT.EXE & MATCLI.EXE	MATCLI.EXE is the Motive Assistant Command Line Interface that gathers system and personal information into a log file. SILENT.EXE executes matcli.exe quietly in the background. Required for accessing Compaq's Help and Support program.
Compaq Video CD Watcher	Compaq MPEG viewer. (Not mandatory)
CompaqPrinTray or PRINTRAY.EXE	Puts printer icon in toolbar. If disabled, the Control Program or Printer Driver can no longer be directly accessed from your desktop.

Program or File Name	Description
CompaqSystray or CPQPSCP.EXE	Compaq system tray icon. (Not mandatory)
COMSMDEXE	3Com utilities. (Not mandatory)
ConfigServices	Part of initial setup. (Not mandatory)
CONMGR.EXE	Connection Manager for Earthlink Internet Services. (Not mandatory)
Controller	Starts WinFax Pro. WinFax will not receive incoming faxes automatically unless running. (Not mandatory)
Cookie Crusher or COOKIE.EXE	A utility that gives the user control over which cookies which are accepted by and stored on the system. (Not mandatory)
Cookie Pal or CPBRWTCH.EXE	A utility that gives the user control over which cookies which are accepted by and stored on the system. (Not mandatory)
Cool Desk or CDESK.EXE	A virtual desktop manager. (Not mandatory or particularly useful)
Cool Note or COOL.EXE	An electronic sticky-note program. (Not mandatory)
Corel Desktop Application Director	Function of Corel Office Suite that launches its programs from the toolbar. (Not mandatory)
Corel Registration Reminder	Function of Corel software that nags the user to register with Corel. Useful only to Corel.
CountrySelection or PCTPTT.EXE	A function of certain modem drivers. As long as the modem is installed and enabled, this feature will reappear after being disabled.
CPQA1000.EXE	Software for the Compaq A1000 printer/fax/ scanner. Required for this device to work.
CPQDFWAG	A utility that runs Compaq diagnostics every time the system boots. (Not mandatory)
CPQEASYACC or CPQEADM.EXE or [bttnserv]	Compaq's Easy Access button support. (Not mandatory)
CPQinet or CPQINET.EXE	A function of Compaq Easy Access Button support. Only required if EAB support is desired.
CPQInet Runtime Services	Compaq Easy Access Button support for AOL and CompuServe. (Not mandatory, and useless if you're using another ISP)
CPQINKAG.EXE	Utility for certain Compaq printers that monitors ink usage. (Not mandatory)
cpqns or CPQNPCSS.EXE	A function of Compaq.Net. Not required for those not using this service.
CPQSTUTFIX	A function of certain sound card drivers that cures problems with sound stutter. Required for those sound cards. Do not remove.

continues

Annotated List of MSCONFIG Startup Entries (*continued*)

Program or File Name	Description
CPUFSB or CPUFSB.EXE or [cpufsb]	Utility that allows the user to adjust the motherboard's front side bus speed through the OS. CAUTION: This utility may cause your system to crash or become unstable and certain components may perform erratically or not at all.
CQSCP2PS or CQSCP2P Server	Compaq printer utility. Required for printer to function.
CreateCD or CREATECD.EXE	A function of EZ CD Creator. (Not mandatory)
Creative Lab's AudioHQ or AHQRUN.EXE or AHQTB.EXE	System tray application for SB Live! Environmental Audio Control plug-ins. (Not mandatory)
Creative Lab's Disc Detector	Autodetects a CD-ROM, DVD-ROM, etc. (Not mandatory)
Creative Lab's Program Launcher	Adds a quick-launch bar to the top of the display and a system tray icon. (Not mandatory)
Critical Update	Forces frequent visits to Microsoft's Web site, looking for updates. (Not mandatory and can be annoying)
CSInject.exe	A function of Norton CleanSweep. (Not mandatory)
CTAVTray or CTAVTRAY.EXE	A function of Creative Labs Soundblaster Live! Soundcard driver. Plays the EAX animation on startup and adds a system tray icon for it. (Not mandatory)
CTFMON	Alternative Language input services for Office XP. If you wish to disable this in startup, then Text Services and Speech applets in the Control Panel must be disabled. (Not mandatory)
CTRegRun or CTREGRUN.EXE	A nag reminder to register a Creative Labs product. (Not mandatory and can be annoying)
CTSysVol	A function of Creative Labs sound card driver that adds volume controls to the toolbar. (Not mandatory)
Cybermedia Guard Dog or GDLAUNCH.EXE	A function of McAfee's Internet Guard Dog Software. (Not mandatory)
CyDoor=CD_Load.exe	Spyware. Remove immediately!
Daemon or DAEMON32.EXE	Pre-loads game profiles for MS Sidewinder game controllers (prior to release 2.0). (Not mandatory)
datcheck or DATCHECK.EXE	Keypanic. Trojan horse that remaps the keyboard. Update and run your antivirus software.
Dcomcnfg or DCOMCNFG.EXE	A function of Microsoft Basic. (Not mandatory)

Program or File Name	Description
Imesh Auto Update or WISEUPDT.EXE	Checks for downloadable imesh updates every time an Internet connection is established. Cannot be removed in msconfig. It puts back the checkmark after you remove it.
Imesh or IMESHCLIENT.EXE	Utility that allows user to download files from several targets simultaneously. (Not mandatory)
Incontrol Desktop MGR or DMHKEY.EXE	A function of Intouch Control software that adds an extra tab in the Display properties for the Diamond Multimedia video card extra settings. (Not mandatory)
Instant Access	A function of TextBridge Pro OCR software. (Not mandatory)
IntelProcNumUtility	Disables CPU ID. (Not mandatory)
internat or INTERNAT.EXE	Allows user to toggle between installed keyboard languages. (Not mandatory). NOTE: Can also be added by a virus called Netsnake. If languages were not installed, update and run antivirus software immediately!
Introduction-Registration	PC introduction & registration for Compaq computers. Should run only once. Remove if it remains after initial use.
Iomega Disk Icons	Iomega Zip Tools application. Changes the icon and description associated with an Iomega Zip drive from a generic icon to an Iomega Zip drive icon. (Not mandatory, nor is it useful)
Iomega QuickSync 3 or quicksync3.exe or [quicksync3]	A program used with Iomega drives, QuickSync 3 is intended to protect the user from data loss. (Not mandatory)
Iomega Startup Options or IMGSTART.EXE	Adds right-click context menu selections for a Zip drive. (Not mandatory, but useful)
Iomega Watch	Iomega Zip Tools application. Causes your Zip drive to spin down when not in use and prompts the user for a password when trying to access a write-protected disk. (Not mandatory, but useful)
IOMON98.EXE	A function of PCCILIN Antivirus software that performs real-time virus checks. (Not mandatory, but useful)
IPinst	Gilat rescue (Satellite system restore). For Gilat Communications Internet satellite systems. Required if you have this system. If removed, can cause the system to become unstable and crash unexpectedly.
IrMon	Required when an infrared wireless device is installed.
isdbdc or ISDBDC.EXE	A function of the Compaq dial-up networking wizard. (Not mandatory)
K6CPU.EXE	Identifies and authenticates AMD K6 CPU. (Not mandatory)
Kagou	The KAK virus. Update and run antivirus software immediately.

continues

Annotated List of MSCONFIG Startup Entries (*continued*)

Program or File Name	Description
KAK.HTA	The KAK virus. Update and run antivirus software immediately.
KAK.HTML	The KAK virus. Update and run antivirus software immediately.
Kernel16	The SUB Seven Trojan Virus. Update and run antivirus software immediately.
kernel32=kern32.exe	The W32/Badtrans@MM Virus. Update and run antivirus software immediately.
Keyboard Manager or MMKEYBD.EXE	A function of the keyboard driver for certain HP keyboards. (Not mandatory)
Launchboard or LNCHBRD.EXE	A program that allows the user to customize the keyboard to launch programs or Web sites. (Not mandatory)
Lexmark PrinTray or PRINTRAY.EXE	A Lexmark printer icon. (Not mandatory)
Lexstart or LEXSTART.EXE	Command interpreter for Lexmark printers. Has been known to induce dial-up networking to connect to the Internet. (Not mandatory)
LIU	Function of Logitech Quick Cam driver. (Not mandatory)
Load = OCRAWARE.EXE	A function of OmniPage Limited Edition that allows the user to scan directly into most word processor applications. (Not mandatory)
Load WebCheck or LOADWC.EXE	Program that manages adding, removing, and updating subscriptions. (Not mandatory)
Loadblackd or BLACKD.EXE	A function of BlackICE Defender, an intrusion detection product. Required if you want to use the product.
LoadPowerProfile	Only required if you are using Windows Power Management through Control Panel. If so, there will be two instances. One is loaded by Machine Run and the other by Machines Services. Do not uncheck one unless you uncheck both. (Not mandatory unless Power Management is enabled.)
LOADQM	MSN Explorer Query Manager. (Not mandatory)
Loadqm	Loads the MSN Explorer Query Manager. (Not mandatory)
Logitech ImageWare Control Center	Function of Logitech Pagescan scanner driver. (Not mandatory)
Logitech Wakeup or LGWAKEUP.EXE	Function of Logitech autofeed scanners. Detects insertion of paper into scanner and launches scanner software. (Not mandatory, but useful)

Program or File Name	Description
Delay or DELAYRUN.EXE	Allows user to configure certain startup items to launch after Windows has loaded. Gives control of the computer to the user more quickly. (Not mandatory)
Description of Shortcut or EZTART.EXE)	A function of McAfee's Utilities which allows the user to customize the appearance of Windows. (Not mandatory)
DEVLDR16.EXE	A function of Creative Labs sound card drivers that provides audio support for DOS applications. (Not mandatory)
DigiGuide or CLIENT.EXE	Electronic TV guide. (Not mandatory)
Digital Dashboard or DEVGULP.EXE	Control panel for a program called Digital Dashboard. (Not mandatory)
Digital River eBot or DOWNLOA~1.EXE	Utility that monitors system and checks for updates to hardware drivers and software updates when an Internet connection is present. (Not mandatory)
Disc Detector or CTNOTIFY.EXE	A function of Creative Labs sound card drivers that automatically detects when a CD or DVD has been inserted into the drive. (Not mandatory)
Disknag or DISKNAG.EXE	A Dell utility that reminds the user to make backup diskettes. (Not mandatory)
DkService or DKSERVICE.EXE	A function of Executive Software's Diskeeper (a third-party disk defragmenting utility) that schedules unattended maintenance. (Not mandatory)
DMASwitch or CLDMA.EXE	A function of CyberLink PowerDVD software that allows user to toggle on/off DMA functions for CD devices. (Not mandatory)
DMISL	Desktop Management Software for Intel TokenExpress network card software. (Not mandatory)
DMISTART or WIN32SL.EXE	Dell or Intel utility that collects system information for Client Manager for remote management and/or technical support. (Not mandatory)
DNE Binding Watchdog or RUNDLL DNES.DLL or [DnDneCheckBindings]	Deterministic NDIS Extender. Part of Gilat Communications Internet satellite systems. Required if you have this system.
dRMON SmartAgent or SMARTAGT.EXE	A utility that is a part of the 3COM NIC software package. (Not mandatory)
DSS	A function of Brøderbund software. Sends information back to manufacturer when Internet connection is detected. (Not mandatory or useful to anyone but Brøderbund)
DXM6Patch_981116 or P_981116.EXE	CAB file extractor. (Not mandatory)
EACLEAN.EXE	Compaq Easy Access Button support for the keyboard. (Not mandatory)
Eapcisetup	A function of Rockwell RipTide soundcard application software. (Not mandatory)

continues

Annotated List of MSCONFIG Startup Entries (*continued*)

Program or File Name	Description
EarthLink ToolBar 5.0 or ETOOLBAR.EXE	A function of EarthLink Internet software. (Not mandatory)
eFax.com Tray Menu or HOTTRAY.EXE	Automatically launches EFAX Messenger software on startup and creates a system tray icon with menu options. (Not mandatory)
EM_EXEC or EM_EXEC.EXE	Advanced features support for a Logitech mouse. (Not mandatory, but removing it will cause certain Logitech features to become disabled.)
EncartaDictionary Quickshelf or QSHLFED.EXE	Quicklaunch for Encarta Dictionary. (Not mandatory)
ENCMON	Keeps track of the time remaining on a factory-installed free trial for AT&T Internet services. (Not mandatory, and totally useless if you're not using their free trial.)
ENCMONITOR or MONITOR.EXE	A Connect Direct function of the Encompass Monitor. (Not mandatory)
EnsonicMixer STARTER.EXE	A function of Ensonic sound card drivers that puts the Ensonic mixer in system tray. (Not mandatory)
EPSON Background Monitor	Monitors the status of any properly configured Epson printer. Removing does not affect the printer's ability to print. (Not mandatory)
ESSDC.EXE	A function of sound card drivers for sound cards with ESS chipset (notably Ensonic). (Not mandatory)
Etraffic or JAVARUN.EXE	Marketing software installed by a company called TopMoxie. **Remove**.
Event Reminder	A function of Dr. Watson. (Not mandatory)
EWELL.HTM	A virus. Check with your antivirus vendor for updates and run immediately.
Explorer	System file. Must be running.
FatPipe (DHCP)	Internet connection-sharing and caching software. (Not mandatory)
FaxTalk CallControl 6.X or FTCLCTRL.EXE	A function of FaxTalk Communicator software that handles incoming and outgoing calls. (Not mandatory)
FEELitDeviceManager or FEELITDM.EXE	A function of Immersion TouchSense device drivers. Required for these devices to work.
Filterguard or FILTRGRD.EXE	A function of SOS Internet Filtering Software. Required for this software to function properly.
Find Fast	Function of Microsoft Office. Indexes files for faster searches. (Not mandatory)
Fine Print Dispatcher or FPDISP3.EXE	Function of certain Compaq printer drivers. Required for printer to function properly.

Program or File Name	Description
Finish Installing or BBSMAR~1.EXE	A function of Bonzai Buddy that reminds the user that more files are needed to complete installation. (Not mandatory)
Fix-It Av or MEMCHECK.EXE	A function of Trend Micro's Ontrack antivirus software. Required for software to function properly.
FlyswatDesktop or FLYDESK.EXE	A function of a program called Flyswat. (Not mandatory)
FMLITES or FMLITES.EXE	A function of some modems that puts a visual display similar to the lights of an external modem on the toolbar. (Not mandatory)
FTUNINST or FTUNINST.EXE	Fax Talk Messenger Pro uninstall program. (Not mandatory)
Gator or GATOR.EXE	A function of Gator, a form filler and adware application that puts menu items on the tool bar. Somewhat resource intensive. Don't use it if you don't need it. (Not mandatory)
GetRight Tray Icon or GETRIGHT.EXE	A download manager that allows the user to resume interrupted downloads and to manage multiple downloads simultaneously. The freeware version adds spyware, the paid version does not. (Not mandatory, but can be useful. Although the spyware isn't.)
Gilat SOM Enumerator or DLLHOST.EXE	A function of Gilat Communications Internet satellite systems, associated with SkyBlaster modem. Required if you have this system.
GilatFTC or FTC.EXE	A function of Gilat Communications Internet satellite systems, associated with SkyBlaster modem. Required if you have this system.
Go!Zilla Monster Downloads	Adds system tray applet for Go!Zilla Web browser. (Not mandatory)
GuardDogEXE or GDLAUNCH.EXE	A function of McAfee's Internet Guard Dog Software. (Not mandatory)
Guardian or CMGRDIAN.EXE	A function of McAfee's Guardian software that adds a system tray icon. (Not mandatory)
HC Reminder or HC.EXE (Note that HC.EXE can also be the Human Click software)	Compaq software. (Not mandatory)
help=3D	This is the VBS/Pleh@MM virus. Check with your antivirus software for updates and run immediately.
Hidserv or HIDSERV.EXE	Human Interface Device Service. Manages devices connected through the USB bus. (Not mandatory, but useful)
HIDSERV.EXE.RUN	Human Interface Device Server. It is required only if you are using USB Audio Devices. (Not mandatory)
Hotbar	Third-party utility that adds new skins for IE. (Not mandatory)

continues

Annotated List of MSCONFIG Startup Entries (*continued*)

Program or File Name	Description
HotSync	Palm synchronization manager. (Not mandatory and should be launched manually)
HP JetDiscovery	A function of HP JetAdmin software that manages network print jobs.
HP Lamp	Utility for certain HP scanners that controls the light source. Required for these scanners to function properly.
HP ScanPicture	Adds a "Scan Picture" option to the File menu of certain applications. If disabled, the menu option will disappear, but the scanner will still function when accessed through the Start menu. (Not mandatory)
Hpha1mon or HPHA1MON.EXE	Driver for the media card reader for certain HP printers that support that function. Required if you wish to use that function.
hppswrsev	Utility for certain HP scanners. (Not mandatory)
hpsysdrv or SPSYSDRV.EXE	A function of the HP keyboard manager that identifies the system as being an HP. On some models, deselecting this function can prevent the system from booting.
HPSCANMonitor or HPSJVXD.EXE	HP scanning software that redirects scanned images from the scanner to the application. Required for the scanner to work properly.
Hpscanpatch or HPSCANFIX.EXE	A driver patch for certain HP scanners. Required for the scanner to work properly.
HumanClick or HC.EXE (Note that HC.EXE can also be the HC Reminder)	A program called HumanClick which allows the user to communicate with visitors on a Web site and to monitor the visitor's activities. (Not mandatory)
HWinst	Gilat rescue (Satellite system restore). For Gilat Communications Internet satellite systems. Required if you have this system. If removed, can cause the system to become unstable and crash unexpectedly.
ICONFIG.EXE or ICONFIG.EXE or [iconfig]	A function of the Superdisk driver. Required for the device to work properly.
ICQ NetDetect Agent	Periodically checks for Internet connectivity. If found, automatically launches ICQ. (Not mandatory and can be quite annoying)
ICSMGR	Monitors DNS and DHCP requests for Internet Connection Sharing (ICS). Required if ICS is installed.
Image & Restore or IMAGE32.EXE	A function of McAfee Nuts & Bolts. Allows a drive to be recovered after an accidental erasure or formatting. (Not mandatory, but extremely useful when you need it!)

Program or File Name	Description
Imesh Auto Update or WISEUPDT.EXE	Checks for downloadable imesh updates every time an Internet connection is established. Cannot be removed in msconfig. It puts back the checkmark after you remove it.
Imesh or IMESHCLIENT.EXE	Utility that allows user to download files from several targets simultaneously. (Not mandatory)
Incontrol Desktop MGR or DMHKEY.EXE	A function of Intouch Control software that adds an extra tab in the Display properties for the Diamond Multimedia video card extra settings. (Not mandatory)
Instant Access	A function of TextBridge Pro OCR software. (Not mandatory)
IntelProcNumUtility	Disables CPU ID. (Not mandatory)
internat or INTERNAT.EXE	Allows user to toggle between installed keyboard languages. (Not mandatory). NOTE: Can also be added by a virus called Netsnake. If languages were not installed, update and run antivirus software immediately!
Introduction-Registration	PC introduction & registration for Compaq computers. Should run only once. Remove if it remains after initial use.
Iomega Disk Icons	Iomega Zip Tools application. Changes the icon and description associated with an Iomega Zip drive from a generic icon to an Iomega Zip drive icon. (Not mandatory, nor is it useful)
Iomega QuickSync 3 or quicksync3.exe or [quicksync3]	A program used with Iomega drives, QuickSync 3 is intended to protect the user from data loss. (Not mandatory)
Iomega Startup Options or IMGSTART.EXE	Adds right-click context menu selections for a Zip drive. (Not mandatory, but useful)
Iomega Watch	Iomega Zip Tools application. Causes your Zip drive to spin down when not in use and prompts the user for a password when trying to access a write-protected disk. (Not mandatory, but useful)
IOMON98.EXE	A function of PCCILIN Antivirus software that performs real-time virus checks. (Not mandatory, but useful)
IPinst	Gilat rescue (Satellite system restore). For Gilat Communications Internet satellite systems. Required if you have this system. If removed, can cause the system to become unstable and crash unexpectedly.
IrMon	Required when an infrared wireless device is installed.
isdbdc or ISDBDC.EXE	A function of the Compaq dial-up networking wizard. (Not mandatory)
K6CPU.EXE	Identifies and authenticates AMD K6 CPU. (Not mandatory)
Kagou	The KAK virus. Update and run antivirus software immediately.

continues

Annotated List of MSCONFIG Startup Entries (*continued*)

Program or File Name	Description
KAK.HTA	The KAK virus. Update and run antivirus software immediately.
KAK.HTML	The KAK virus. Update and run antivirus software immediately.
Kernel16	The SUB Seven Trojan Virus. Update and run antivirus software immediately.
kernel32=kern32.exe	The W32/Badtrans@MM Virus. Update and run antivirus software immediately.
Keyboard Manager or MMKEYBD.EXE	A function of the keyboard driver for certain HP keyboards. (Not mandatory)
Launchboard or LNCHBRD.EXE	A program that allows the user to customize the keyboard to launch programs or Web sites. (Not mandatory)
Lexmark PrinTray or PRINTRAY.EXE	A Lexmark printer icon. (Not mandatory)
Lexstart or LEXSTART.EXE	Command interpreter for Lexmark printers. Has been known to induce dial-up networking to connect to the Internet. (Not mandatory)
LIU	Function of Logitech Quick Cam driver. (Not mandatory)
Load = OCRAWARE.EXE	A function of OmniPage Limited Edition that allows the user to scan directly into most word processor applications. (Not mandatory)
Load WebCheck or LOADWC.EXE	Program that manages adding, removing, and updating subscriptions. (Not mandatory)
Loadblackd or BLACKD.EXE	A function of BlackICE Defender, an intrusion detection product. Required if you want to use the product.
LoadPowerProfile	Only required if you are using Windows Power Management through Control Panel. If so, there will be two instances. One is loaded by Machine Run and the other by Machines Services. Do not uncheck one unless you uncheck both. (Not mandatory unless Power Management is enabled.)
LOADQM	MSN Explorer Query Manager. (Not mandatory)
Loadqm	Loads the MSN Explorer Query Manager. (Not mandatory)
Logitech ImageWare Control Center	Function of Logitech Pagescan scanner driver. (Not mandatory)
Logitech Wakeup or LGWAKEUP.EXE	Function of Logitech autofeed scanners. Detects insertion of paper into scanner and launches scanner software. (Not mandatory, but useful)

Program or File Name	Description
Lotus Organizer Easy Clip	Function of Lotus Organizer. Collects information from sources such as email to create an Organizer address, appointment, task or Notepad page. (Not mandatory)
Lotus Quick Start	Control pad for Lotus SmartSuite. (Not mandatory)
Lotus Suite Start	Start icons for Lotus SmartSuite that appear on the taskbar when you start Windows. Removing this item can result in error messages and prevent SmartSuite from working properly.
LS120 Superdisk	Disk caching utility for LS-120. (Not mandatory)
LVComs or LVCOMS.EXE	Function of the Logitech QuickCam driver. (Not mandatory)
Lwinst Run Profiler or LWTEST.EXE or LWEMON.EXE	Function of the Logitech Wingman joystick driver. (Not mandatory)
LXSUPMON (LXSUPMON.EXE)	Function of Lexmark printer driver. (Not mandatory)
Machine Debug Manager or mdm	Part of Visual Studio 6.0. This is required only if a second machine is used to debug programs under development on current computer. (Not mandatory)
MapNDrive or MAPNDRIVE.EXE	A third-party scripting tool that manages mapped network drives. Needed if installed.
Matrox Powerdesk	A function of Matrox graphics card drivers that allows users to adjust display settings on the fly. (Not mandatory)
McAfee Guardian or CMGRDIAN.EXE	A function of McAfee Uninstaller software. Automatically identifies and removes the unnecessary files that remain after a program is removed. (Not mandatory)
McAfee Image or IMAGE32.EXE	A function of McAfee Image that creates an image snapshot of the critical sectors on your hard drive. In the event these sectors become corrupted, Image uses the snapshot to restore data. (Not mandatory)
McAfee VirusScan Registration	Function of McAfee VirusScan that nags the user to register the product. (Not mandatory)
McAfee Wingauge	A McAfee utility that monitors system performance. (Not mandatory)
McAfeeVirusScanService or AVSYNMGR.EXE	A function of McAfee VirusScan version 5.x that runs all the functions within a single environment. (Not mandatory, but useful)
McAfeeWebScanX or WEBSCANX.EXE or [Webscanx]	A McAfee utility that monitors Internet activity for possibly harmful events. (Not mandatory, but useful)

continues

Annotated List of MSCONFIG Startup Entries (*continued*)

Program or File Name	Description
MDAC_RUNONCE or RUNONCE.EXE	Microsoft Data Access Components Run Once Wrapper. This is required for Microsoft Data Access Components. Run Once refers to once per session and therefore appears any time a MDAC app is running.
MediaRing Talk or MRTALK.EXE	Voice recognition software. Resource intensive. Remove if not needed.
Memturbo	A shareware program that monitors memory usage and dumps code no longer in use. (Not mandatory)
MGAVRTCL.EXE or MGAVRTCL.EXE	A function McAfee Antivirus. Required for real-time virus scanning.
MicroAngelo Desktop	Preloads certain files critical to MicroAngelo 5.0 to facilitate faster loading. (Not mandatory)
Microsoft Critical Update	Detects and installs critical updates from the Microsoft site when an Internet connection is present. (Not mandatory)
Microsoft Find Fast	A service of Microsoft Office. Indexes files on your hard drive for faster search. (Not mandatory)
Microsoft Greetings Reminders	Reminder of special events like birthdays. (Not mandatory).
Microsoft Office Startup	Preloads certain .DLL files to speed up the launch of Microsoft Office. Also places icon in system tray. (Not mandatory)
Microsoft Sidewinder Game Controller Software	Preloads profiles for games. (Not mandatory)
Microsoft Webserver	Personal Web server program. (Not mandatory)
Microsoft Works Calendar	MS Works program provides notifications when dates on the MS Works Calendar are reached. (Not mandatory)
Microsoft Works Calendar Reminders	MS Works Calendar reminder. (Not mandatory)
Microsoft Works Portfolio, WorksFUD, Microsoft Update Detection, Cal reminder shortcut	These are used by Works 2001. Check for updates and announce reminders that were configured in Works programs. (Not mandatory)
Microsoft Works Update Detection	Detects and installs MS Works updates from the Microsoft site. (Not mandatory)
MINIFERT.EXE	Electronic distribution software bundled with certain Compaq computers. (Not mandatory)
Minilog or MINILOG.EXE	A function of ZoneAlarm firewall software that maintains the event log. Required for software to function properly.
Mirabilis ICQ	Automatically starts up ICQ when Internet connection is detected. (Not mandatory)

Program or File Name	Description
Mixghost	Management utility for Altec Lansing speakers. (Not mandatory)
mmtray	Places a Music Box Jukebox icon in the system tray. (Not mandatory)
MoneyAgent or MONEY EXPRESS.EXE	Function of Microsoft Money. (Not mandatory)
MOSEARCH	Similar to Find Fast feature in Office 2000. Uses the Indexing Services in Office XP to create a catalog of Office files on your computer's hard disk. (Not mandatory)
MotiveMonitor (motmon.exe)	A function of HP Instant Support that watches for errors and collects information useful for resolution through the Internet and email. (Not mandatory, but useful)
Mount Safe & Sound	A function of McAfee VirusScan version 5.x that creates back-up sets of critical files in a separate area of a hard drive. (Not mandatory)
MS Money Startup	Launches Microsoft Money. (Not mandatory)
MSKernel32 or WINDOWS\SYSTEM\MSKernel32.vbs	The LOVE-LETTER-FOR-YOU virus. Update and run antivirus software immediately.
MSMSGS or MSMSGS.EXE or MSN Messenger	MSN Instant Messenger Service. (Not mandatory)
MSNQuickView	MSN Toolbar that launches at startup.
Mstask	A Microsoft scheduling agent that can be configured to run several applications at specified times. (Not mandatory)
MSUser32 or WINDOWS\SYSTEM\MSUser32.vbs	The LOOK.VBS virus. Update and run antivirus software immediately.
NAV defalert	Norton Antivirus Definitions Alert. A function of Norton Antivirus that warns the user when AV signature files are outdated. (Not mandatory, but useful)
Nav_setup or NAV_SE~1.EXE	McAfee Installation Wizard. Indicates that software installation was not completed. Run setup program again or remove.
Ndetect	Automatically detects Internet connection and launches ICQ. (Not mandatory)
NeoPlanet or NEO.EXE	Starts Neoplanet web browser automatically when in Startup and creates a system tray icon that allows the user to access its options. (Not mandatory)
Netsonic or WEBMAIN.EXE	Internet caching program. (Not mandatory).
Netword Agent NWANT33.EXE	Internet browsing utility that allows single-word Web searches. (Not mandatory)
NETWORK.VBS	NETWORK.VBS virus. Update antivirus software and run immediately.
NetworkSetup or DLINK.EXE	A DLink driver utility that provides shortcuts to DLink Web sites. (Not mandatory)

continues

Annotated List of MSCONFIG Startup Entries (*continued*)

Program or File Name	Description
Netzero or NZSTART.EXE	Automatically launches Netzero ISP software at bootup. (Not mandatory)
NetZip Smart Downloader	A download utility that adds Pause, Resume, and Reconnect to your downloads. (Not mandatory)
Norton AutoProtect	Norton Antivirus program. Scans for viruses when you open a program or file. (Not mandatory, but useful)
Norton Crashguard Monitor	Function of Norton Utilities that keeps renegade applications from crashing system. Causes instability with WinMe. (Not mandatory)
Norton Email Protect	Function of Norton Antivirus that sets up a proxy server to isolate the main system from email-borne viruses. (Not mandatory)
Norton System Doctor	Norton program that monitors system configuration and alerts the user when the configuration changes in ways that may cause problems. (Not mandatory)
NovastorScheduler	A function of NovaStor NovaBACKUP Software. Required for unattended scheduled backups.
NPROTECT	A function of Norton Utilities. Protects files in Recycle Bin. (Not mandatory)
nscheck or NSCHECK.EXE	Internet caching software. Has been known to cause problems with certain ISPs. (Not mandatory)
oadaemon or OADAEMON.EXE or [oadaemon]	Function of the Compaq C3-1000 printer. Required for printer to function properly.
OEMCLEANUP or OEM_RESET.EXE	Resets OEM installation settings at each bootup. Useful if you want all computers in an organization to be consistent. (Not mandatory)
Office Startup or OSA.EXE	Preloads certain files for quicker launching of Office applications. (Not mandatory)
Onflow or UNINSTALL ONFLOW.EXE	Onflow is software that places advertising banners in certain types of software. This program can be run to remove it. (Not mandatory)
Operator	Function of Media Pilot software. Locks port open. (Not mandatory)
Pagekeeper Jobs	Function of Pagekeeper scanner software that manages documents. (Not mandatory)
Password Pal or PASSPAL.EXE	A utility that stores all passwords associated to a to a specific user in encrypted form. (Not mandatory)
PC Health or PCHSCHD.EXE	WinMe only. Required for the System Restore utility to function properly in Windows Me. The program takes a snapshot of the registry and places the information into data archive.

Program or File Name

Description

PCTVOICE or PCTVOICE.EXE	PCTVoice is a program used by certain modems for video conferencing. (Not mandatory)
Pe2ckfnt SE or CHKFONT.EXE	A function of Ulead Photo Express that confirms whether or not fonts are installed properly on a computer. (Not mandatory)
Photo Express Calender Checker SE	A function of Ulead Photo Express that configures Weekly/Monthly/Yearly calendars as wallpaper. (Not mandatory)
PiDunHk or PIDUNHK.EXE	A function of Prodigy Internet services. (Not mandatory)
PiStartup or PISTARTUP.EXE	A function of Prodigy Internet services. (Not mandatory)
Pointer POINT32.EXE	Function of the Microsoft Intellipoint mouse software. If not loaded, then the wheel may not work in certain applications. (Not mandatory, but useful)
Power Meter	Utility on Dell laptop for battery strength and AC power source for batteries. It can be manually launched when it is needed.
Power Panel plus or PANPLUS.EXE or [Panplus]	A function of PowerPanel Plus software (included (included with CyberPower's Power99 and Power2000 models of UPS). Monitors condition and charge of UPS and performs automatic shutdown of system in the event of power failure. Required for full functionality.
Power Reg Scheduler	Software registration reminder. (Not mandatory)
pp5300USB	A function of Paperport software that monitors the status of a Visioneer OneTouch 5300 scanner. (Not mandatory)
Primax 3D Mouse	Driver support for Primax mouse. (Not mandatory)
PROMON.EXE	Part of Intel NIC diagnostics. (Not mandatory)
Prpcui	Dell utility which manages Intel's Speed-Step functions. (Not mandatory)
Ptsnoop.exe	A function of several modem drivers that monitors the COM port. Will automatically reset itself as long as the modem is enabled.
Q shlf or Quick Shelf or ENCICONS.EXE or [qshlfed]	Launches Encarta dictionary program. (Not mandatory)
Qagent	Quicken Download Manager (also known as Qagent). When the Quicken Download Manager option is enabled, it takes advantage of unused bandwidth on an Internet connection to download current financial information any time your computer is connected to the Internet. (Not mandatory)
QBCD autorun	Automatically launches Quickbooks. (Not mandatory)
QD FastAndSafe	Function of Norton CleanSweep. Deletes unnecessary files. Best if run manually. (Not mandatory)
QuickenSEMessage	A messaging option for Quicken software. (Not mandatory)

continues

Annotated List of MSCONFIG Startup Entries (*continued*)

Program or File Name	Description
QuickShelf 99	Places an icon in the system tray for launching Microsoft Bookshelf. (Not mandatory)
RamBooster or RAMBOOSTER.EXE	A utility that monitors memory usage and dumps unnecessary code. (Not mandatory)
Rave 2 or RAVE.EXE	A Windows application that allows voice communication over an Internet connection. (Not mandatory)
Real Jukebox Systray	Function of Real Jukebox software. Allows user to launch Real Jukebox by double clicking on the icon in the system tray, and periodically checks for an Internet connection in order to download updates. (Not mandatory)
RealTray REALPLAY.EXE	Function of Real Audio software. Allows user to launch Real Jukebox by double clicking on the icon in the system tray, and periodically checks for an Internet connection in order to download updates. (Not mandatory)
Refresh	A function of Iomega Zip drives. (Not mandatory)
Register Drop Handler	A utility for managing images created by digital cameras or scanners. (Not mandatory)
Regtrk	A function of Norton Utilities that monitors changes to the registry. (Not mandatory, but useful)
Reminder	Bill payment reminder function of MS Money. (Not mandatory)
Reminder-cpqXXXXX or REMIND32.EXE	Reminder to register a Compaq printer. (Not mandatory)
RFTray	Launches the Reality Fusion GameCam Video Interaction Technology Software that ships with the Logitech QuickCam (and other) PC video cameras. (Not mandatory)
Ring Central Fax	Utility for allowing PC to answer faxes. (Not mandatory)
rnaapp	Application required by Dial-Up Networking. It loads when a connection is initiated.
Run = (WINDOWS \SYSTEM\list.vbs)	The LIST.VBS virus. Update antivirus software and run immediately.
RUN=	Identifies a specific program to be run during startup. A large number of RUN= statements which are not followed by a specific command may indicate a virus infection.
RUN= (TEMP\LIST.VBS)	The LIST.VBS virus. Update and run antivirus software immediately.
RUN=HPFSCHED	Nags user to register HP printer or scanner. (Not mandatory and can be annoying)

Program or File Name	Description
RUNDLL32.EXE	Runs individual routines that have been packaged into a .DLL file. (Not mandatory)
SA3DSRV	Windows 3D sound extension added by Aureal 3D sound cards. (Not mandatory)
SAFEINST.EXE	A utility from Imation that is part of the LS120 Superdisk setup. It checks the parallel port chipset for compatibility. No longer required once software is installed and drive is working.
Savenow or SAVENOW.EXE	A spyware utility that transmits user information to specified locations on the Internet. **Remove**.
SCANREG	Makes a copy of the Windows Registry after attempted startup. Designates whether startup was successful or not. Useful for backing up in the event of a corrupted registry. Does not remain in memory after the backup has been generated. **While not mandatory, registry backups will not be generated if removed. Do not remove!**
ScanRegistry (WINDOWS\list.vbs)	The LIST.VBS virus. Update and run antivirus software immediately.
ScanRegistry or SCANREGW.EXE	This is the legitimate registry scanning utility and must be run at startup. Without it, backup copies of the registry are not completed.
Scheduling Agent	Function of Task Scheduler that automates scheduled events. (Not mandatory if scheduled events are not used)
Service Connection or SCCENTER.EXE	A utility installed by Backweb software for monitoring the connection status. (Not mandatory)
ShockmachineReminder or SMREMINDER.EXE	A utility installed by Shockwave software that monitors the Shockwave Web site for software updates and new content. (Not mandatory)
SHPC32	A function of a Compaq printer driver. Required for the printer to work properly.
SKA.EXE=SKA.EXE	The Happy99.Worm. Not likely to be seen now. If found, run antivirus software immediately.
Sm56acl	System tray icon added by SM56 modem driver installation. (Not mandatory)
SMS Client Service	Starts the Microsoft Systems Management Server client software. You can remove it, but you might get fired.
SMS Win9x Message Agent	Systems Management Server utility that directs messages to a specific server.
Snsicon or SNSICON.EXE	A utility installed by Second Nature Software, a program that changes background wallpaper based on a preconfigured schedule. Only required if you want the wallpaper to change.
Sonic A3D Control or VRTXCTRL.EXE	Management software for Sonic A3D sound cards. Not mandatory)

continues

Annotated List of MSCONFIG Startup Entries (*continued*)

Program or File Name	Description
SpeedRacer	A utility installed by Creative Labs sound card software. (Not mandatory)
Spinner Plus or SPINNER.EXE	A utility that provides access to Web-based music broadcasts. (Not mandatory)
SS Runner V3.0 or RUNNER.EXE	Synthesoft screensaver software that creates a system tray icon which enables the screensaver and provides access to its option menus. (Not mandatory)
Sspdsrv or SSDPSRV.EXE	WinMe. Plug 'n Play function that provides Simple Service Discovery Protocol (SSDP) and General Event Notification Architecture (GENA) support.
Startacc or STARTACC.EXE	Internet caching software. Part of Webroot Accelerate 2000. (Not mandatory)
Startup	A function of Iomega Zip drive software. (Not mandatory)
Startupmonitor	A freeware tool that adds itself to your startup menu so that it can warn you whenever another program tries the same stunt.
State Manager or StateMgr or STATEMGR.EXE	WinMe only. Takes a snapshot of the registry and places the information into data archive. Required for Restore functionality. Do not remove.
StillImageMonitor or STIMON.EXE	A utility that moderates transfer of data between USB still image devices and the application. Consists of two modules, Event Monitor and Control Center. Event Monitor detects events from connected USB scanning devices, while Control Center determines how to react to these incoming events. (Not mandatory, but is included with certain HP scanners. If included, then it must be running for your scanning software to work properly.)
Sxgdsenu or SXGDSENU.EXE	On some laptop computers, it is installed to manage sleep or hibernation functions of power management. If your laptop installed it, then you need it.
SymTray - Norton SystemWorks	Collects all Norton SystemWorks system tray icons together into a single icon. (Not mandatory)
SynTPEnh or SYNTPENH.EXE and SynTPLpr or SYNTPLPR.EXE	On some laptop computers, it is installed to manage the touchpad. If your laptop installed it, then you need it.
Sysdoc or SYSDOC32.EXE	Automatic startup for Norton System Doctor. Best if run manually. (Not mandatory)
System DLF or CPQDIAGA.EXE	A Compaq diagnostic utility, which allows the user to view information about the computer's hardware and software configuration. (Not mandatory)
SystemBackup = C:\WINDOWS\MTX_.EXE	The W95.MTX virus/worm. Obsolete, but occasionally reappears. Run antivirus software immediately.

Program or File Name	Description
SystemTray or SYSTRAY.EXE	Windows system tray. This is the system utility that manages all this mess I'm discussing here. Required.
SystemWizard Sniffer	A hardware/software diagnostics utility from SystemSoft. (Not mandatory)
SYSTRAY	Manages the Start button and taskbar region of the screen. No point in removing it. It'll just come back.
T4UMHF5=C:\WINDOWS \TEMP\T4UMHF5.VBS	The VBS/Anjulie@MM Virus. Update antivirus software and run immediately.
Taskbar Display Controls	Appears if the graphics card driver inserts Display Settings icon in the system tray. (Not mandatory)
TaskMonitor or TASKMON.EXE	Microsoft utility which monitors program usage. (Not mandatory)
TCAUTIEXE or TCAUDIAG	A diagnostics utility for 3COM NICs. Monitors status of network connection. (Not mandatory)
Time Sync Add Client	For Palms and PDAs, needed in the startup in order for those devices to function properly.
Timemanager.exe	A utility that monitors how much actual time is spent on any given activity. (Not mandatory)
Tips	Pop-up pointers for an Intellipoint mouse. (Not mandatory)
Touch Manager	A keyboard utility. (Not mandatory)
Tour or WINCOOL.EXE	WinMe. A popup that nags at user to watch the Windows Millennium Interactive Video Sampler. (Not mandatory and quite annoying)
Tray Temperature or WEATHERBUG.EXE or [Weatherbug]	A utility that links to the Weatherbug Web site and provides up-to-the-minute weather forecasts. (Not mandatory)
Trayzip or TRAYZIP.EXE	A Zip compression utility that creates a system tray icon. (Not mandatory)
Trickler or FSG.EXE	A spyware program that collects information from the computer and transmits it to a preconfigured Internet location. **Remove**.
TrueVector or VSMON.EXE	A function of ZoneAlarm firewall software. Required for the software to work properly.
TVWakeup	Function of Microsoft Web TV that provides controls on the taskbar. (Not mandatory)
TweakDUN	A utility that fine-tunes certain Windows settings in order to maximize efficiency of bandwidth usage on a Dial-up Networking connection. (Not mandatory, but useful)
TweakUI	TweakUI is a program available from Microsoft's Web site that allows a user to adjust many features not otherwise adjustable. Most options require the program to load at startup in order to effect the changes. When TweakUI is used to enter a network password, it will be listed twice. If you remove one, you should remove both. (Not mandatory)

continues

Annotated List of MSCONFIG Startup Entries (*continued*)

Program or File Name	Description
USB Hub Keyboard Patch or SKBPATCH.EXE	Win95. USB driver update that extends support to USB keyboards. Required for Win95 users wanting to use a USB keyboard.
USBMMKBD	Utility that provides USB keyboard support. Required on most system using USB keyboards.
User32DLL (WINDOWS\User32DLL.vbs)	The LOOK.vbs virus. Update antivirus software and run immediately.
USRobotics online registration	Registration nag for owners of US Robotics products. (Not mandatory and quite annoying)
VidSvr	TV guide for WEBTV users. (Not mandatory)
VirusScan Console	A function of McAfee VirusScan (through version 4.x) used for scheduling unattended virus scans. Not required if you don't perform regularly scheduled scans.
VirusScan System Scan	A function of McAfee VirusScan (through version 4.x). Known to interfere with certain programs. Scan files manually. (Not mandatory)
VirusScan System Tray	A function of McAfee VirusScan (through version 4.x). Runs if you have any of the VirusScan options running.
Vistascan or VISTASCAN.EXE	Function of VistaScan scanner software. Click this icon and a menu opens. (Not mandatory)
Voodoo2 or 3DFXV2PS.DLL	Function of the Voodoo 2 graphics adapters. Restores Voodoo 2 registry settings that can't be retained normally. Required for 3dfx/Voodoo2 owners.
VortexTray	System tray application for Aureal Vortex-based soundcards. (Not mandatory)
VoyetraTray	Function of Turtle Beach Montego II (and other) sound card drivers. Provides Control Group for the sound functions associated with AudioStation 3 and 32. (Not mandatory)
VS_STAT.EXE; VSECOMR.EXE; VSHWIN32.EXE; VSSTAT.EXE	Part of McAfee antivirus program. Required for automated scanning of files and for scheduled system scans.
Vshield	A function of McAfee Antivirus that scans new files as they are added. Not required if manual scans of downloads and disk contents are faithfully done. (Not mandatory, but quite useful)
Vshwin32EXE or VSHWIN32.EXE	A 32-bit function of McAfee Antivirus that scans new files as they are added. Not required if manual scans of downloads and disk contents are faithfully done. (Not mandatory, but quite useful)

Program or File Name	Description
VsStatEXE or VSSTAT.EXE	A function of McAfee Antivirus that logs files coming in and actions taken by McAfee on those files. (Not mandatory, but useful)
W3kNETWORK or W3KNET.DLL	A function of advertising-supported software that automatically downloads ads to the users' computers whenever the associated software is run. Quite annoying, but generally required for the associated software to run properly.
Washer or WASHER.EXE	The Windows utility that automatically cleans your browser's cache, cookies, history, mail trash, etc. based on whatever schedule the user has configured in the Clear History function of Internet Options. (Not mandatory, but quite useful)
washindex	A function Webroot Windows Washer, a third-party utility that deletes unnecessary duplicate and temporary files. You can remove it, but as long as the software is installed, it'll just come back.
Watchdog Program or WATCHDOG.EXE	Third-party utility that monitors ISP/dial-up connection. (Not mandatory)
Waterfall Pro 2.99 or WFP.EXE or [wfp]	Waterfall Pro is a utility which monitors CPU temperature and slows CPU speed if it gets too warm. (Not mandatory)
Wcmdmgr.exe	A function of WildTangent software that periodically contacts WildTangent servers to see if an update is available. (Not mandatory)
Web outfitter tray or STTRAY.EXE	Automatically launches Intel's Web Outfitter software at startup and creates a system tray icon for the option menus.
WebHancer Agent or WHAGENT.EXE	System tray for Webhancer software, another Web caching utility. (Not mandatory and extremely resource intensive)
Webshots	A utility that automatically downloads screensavers from the Webshots Web site. Useful only if you have Webshots updating your wallpaper on a daily basis.
WhenUstart.exe or WHENU.EXE	An online shopping service that automatically launches each time you run Windows. (Not mandatory or useful)
Win32DLL =WINDOWS \Win32DLL.vbs	The LOVE-LETTER-FOR-YOU.TXT.VBS virus. Update and run antivirus software immediately.
WinampAgent or WINAMPA.EXE	Launches a system tray icon for Winamp Player software. (Not mandatory)
WIN-BUGSFIX	LOVE-LETTER-FOR-YOU.TXT.vbs virus removal instructions
WINDLL.EXE	The GirlFriend 1.35 virus. Mostly obsolete, but still pops up from time to time. Collects User ID and password information and transmits it to a preconfigured Internet location. Run antivirus software immediately.

continues

Annotated List of MSCONFIG Startup Entries (*continued*)

Program or File Name	Description
Windows Eyes	A utility for blind computer users that replaces common computer responses with speech. (Not mandatory, but useful to those who need it)
Windows=c:\msdos98.exe	The MINE.EXE virus. Update and run antivirus software immediately.
WinFAT32=WinFAT32.EXE	The VBS.Loveletter virus. Update and run antivirus software immediately.
Winkey	Freeware program that allows user to custom-configure Windows hot keys.
WINMGMT.EXE	Enterprise Management software that runs from administrator's machine. Should be removed from client machines.
winmodem or WINMODEM.EXE	Utility installed by a number of software modems. (Not mandatory, but can be useful)
WinPoET or WinPPPoverEthernet.exe or [WinPPPoverEthernet]	Provides endusers with authenticated access to high-speed broadband networks using the Microsoft dial-up interface. (Not mandatory)
WKCALREM	Yet another Microsoft Works Calendar reminder. (Not mandatory)
WKDETECT	Automatically looks for updates for Microsoft Works when Internet connection is present. (Not mandatory and can be annoying)
WKFUD.EXE	Microsoft marketing drivel. (Not mandatory or useful)
Yahoo Pager or YPAGER.EXE	A function of Yahoo! Messenger that allows the user to send instant messages. (Not mandatory)
zBrowser Launcher or COMMANDR.EXE or ITOUCH.EXE	Function of Logitech keyboard software that creates a system tray icon which the user can access the menu options. From here, the user can program certain keys on Logitech keyboards. (Not mandatory)
ZipDisk Icons	Related to the Zip drive. (Not mandatory)
ZoneAlarm (zonealarm.exe)	Launches ZoneAlarm at startup and creates a system tray icon from which you can access the menu options. Required for ZoneAlarm to function properly. Uses 7% resources

Table 7.4: While not a complete listing (I'm not sure that would be possible), these are some of the more commonly seen Startup options in MSCONFIG.

One of the most feared events for most Windows users is the infamous Blue Screen of Death. Microsoft prefers to call it simply the Stop Screen for some reason. Not quite as descriptive or as accurate as the BSOD, in my opinion. Most people swear a bit and shut their machines off, hoping against hope that they will successfully reboot.

Don't be so hasty to restart your machine before reading the information. The BSOD actually contains some valuable information in the line that begins "STOP =". While there are probably a hundred or more stop codes in Microsoft's database, only a few appear that often. I'm only including the "most popular," in **Table 7.5**.

For more information on Inside the Blue Sceen of Death, go to page 703, Chapter 27 of *The Complete Guide to A+ Certification.*

Windows Stop Codes

STOP CODE (0's after X truncated)	DESCRIPTION	POSSIBLE SOLUTION
0x00A: IRQL_NOT_LESS_OR_EQUAL	A process or driver tried to access a memory address for which it did not have permission.	Can be caused by hardware or software. Often is anomalous event. Restart the machine. If error does not resolve, uninstall any new hardware that was installed. If no new hardware was installed, it may point to bad memory.
0x00A5: ACPI_BIOS_ERROR	The computer's Advanced Configuration and Power Interface BIOS is not compatible with the OS.	Upgrade the system BIOS or make sure that power management is turned off in both the BIOS and the OS.
0x00B4: VIDEO_DRIVER_INIT_FAILURE	The video card could not be initialized.	There could be a hardware conflict with the video card. Start in safe mode and roll back all recently installed drivers, then reconfigure the video card.
0x00F2: HARDWARE_INTERRUPT_STORM	An Interrupt Storm has occurred.	A level-triggered device has failed to release the interrupt after an I/O operation and is now barraging the system with interrupt calls it doesn't need. A corrupted driver usually causes this. Start in Safe Mode and scan all devices in Device Manager.

continues

Windows Stop Codes (*continued*)

STOP CODE (0's after X truncated)	DESCRIPTION	POSSIBLE SOLUTION
0x001: APC_INDEX_MISMATCH	Mismatch of thread and asynchronous procedure call (APC) indexes.	Usually occurs after installing new equipment. Try restarting machine. If it blue-screens again, remove the equipment, boot to Last Known Good.
0x001A: MEMORY_MANAGEMENT	The MMC was unable to read and/or write to locations in memory.	Almost always points to bad memory.
0x001E: KMODE_EXCEPTION_NOT_HANDLED	CPU encountered an event it didn't know how to handle. A device driver attempted an illegal function.	Generally hardware related. If this occurs after installing new equipment, try restarting machine. If it blue-screens again, remove the equipment, boot to Last Known Good. If no new equipment was installed, run hardware diagnostics.
0x002: DEVICE_QUEUE_NOT_BUSY	A device queue that should be showing activity is dormant.	If this occurs after installing new equipment, try restarting machine. If it blue-screens again, remove the equipment, boot to Last Known Good.
0x002E: DATA_BUS_ERROR	System memory parity error.	Generally points to defective memory. However, since it can point to bad RAM, bad video memory, or bad L2 cache, it can be hard to pinpoint.
0x003: INVALID_AFFINITY_SET	Indicates a null of an improper subset affinity. (Programming error)	If this occurs after installing new equipment, try restarting machine. If it blue-screens again, remove the equipment, boot to Last Known Good. Can also suggest a memory error.
0x005A: CRITICAL_SERVICE_FAILED	A kernel service failed to start during initialization.	Can be anomalous. Can be the result of newly installed hardware. Can be the result of corrupted files. If hardware is recently installed, you know the drill. For others, restart, using Last Known Good.

STOP CODE (0's after X truncated)	DESCRIPTION	POSSIBLE SOLUTION
0x006F: SESSION3_INITIALIZATION_FAILED	Windows Executive failed to initialize.	A corrupt device driver can cause this, as can a failure of the file system to properly initialize. Start using Last Known Good.
0x007: INVALID_SOFTWARE_INTERRUPT	An IRQ call outside of the range of software was attempted.	Rare message. Usually accompanies older software installed on a modern OS. However, it can also show up with hardware installations. If new hardware was just installed, remove it and reboot. Reinstall the hardware and try again. If the blue screen recurs, you can't use that device.
0x007: UNEXPECTED_KERNEL_MODE_TRAP	Almost always a CPU failure.	Subsequent parameters indicate exact failure. Most are programming errors. Restart the machine.
0x007A: KERNEL_DATA_INPAGE_ERROR	Data required by the system kernel is in the paging file and cannot be read back.	This one's no fun. Disk controller drivers may have failed. Or there may be a hardware failure. Restart the machine using Last Known Good.
0x007B: INACCESSIBLE_BOOT_DEVICE	The system partition or boot volume could not be read during boot.	Often the result of installing incorrect drivers after a disk or adapter upgrade. May be something as simple as a resource conflict between a new controller card and another device. Can also be caused by a virus.
0x008E : KERNEL_MODE_EXCEPTION_NOT_HANDLED	A kernel application generated an error.	Usually a result of hardware compatibility issues. Can sometimes be resolved with a BIOS upgrade or an updated device driver, if you know what device is causing the problem. Which you rarely do.

continues

Windows Stop Codes (*continued*)

STOP CODE (0's after X truncated)	DESCRIPTION	POSSIBLE SOLUTION
0x009: IRQL_NOT_GREATER_OR_EQUAL	OS was expecting an IRQ different than what it got.	Almost always appears in conjunction with newly installed hardware. Remove it and reboot. Reinstall the hardware and try again. If the blue screen recurs, see if there are updated drivers. If not, give up.
0x009C: MACHINE_CHECK_EXCEPTION	Unrecoverable CPU failure.	Most often is the result of the CPU overheating. Letting the machine cool down will generally allow the machine to restart. Check your cooling fans and make sure you're not overclocking the CPU.
0x009F: DRIVER_POWER_STATE_FAILURE	An event involving a transition in power occurred.	Either an attempt to shut down the system failed, or coming out of stand-by or hibernation failed. Restart the machine and double-check the settings in Power Options.
0x0023: FAT_FILE_SYSTEM	I/O error to a FAT16 or FAT32 drive.	May indicate a physical problem with the hard disk. A badly fragmented drive will also return this error. Drive-mirroring software sometimes returns this error after an I/O error.
0x0024: NTFS_FILE_SYSTEM	I/O error to a NTFS drive.	May indicate a physical problem with the hard disk. A badly fragmented drive will also return this error. Drive-mirroring software sometimes returns this error after an I/O error.
0x0050: PAGE_FAULT_IN_NONPAGED_AREA	Memory read errors.	Generally points to bad RAM.
0x0051: REGISTRY_ERROR	Invalid instruction called from registry.	Registry may be corrupt. Also may indicate a misbehaving device driver. Also a file system malfunction can cause this error.

STOP CODE (0's after X truncated)	DESCRIPTION	POSSIBLE SOLUTION
0x0053: NO_BOOT_DEVICE	BOOT.INI pointed to an invalid system disk.	Can be the result of drive failure. Or a newly installed drive may have changed the drive letters so that BOOT.INI is no longer correctly configured.
0x0059: PINBALL_FILE_SYSTEM	An error in the non-paged memory pool.	A fairly rare message that is usually the result of the computer system not having sufficient RAM. Memory is cheap. Buy more.
0x0077: KERNEL_STACK_INPAGE_ERROR	The paging file could not be read.	The data being read might simply be corrupted. There might be a bad sector on the hard drive. Your system might be infected by a virus. Boot to Safe Mode, run SCANDISK and your antivirus software, and reboot.
0x0079: MISMATCHED_HAL	An incorrect version of HAL.SYS is loading for the configuration.	A system backup of a single-CPU system might be copied to a multi-CPU system (or vice versa). Firmware ACPI might be configured when Windows is installed and then removed later.
0x0080: NMI_HARDWARE_FAILURE	A nonmaskable interrupt occurred which the CPU did not know how to handle.	Definite hardware failure. It's usually related to memory. However, if new hardware was installed, uninstall everything and start again. If not, pull out the diagnostics software and give the system a complete test.
0xC009A: STATUS_INSUFFICIENT_RESOURCES	All memory in the paged pool has been used up.	Check to see how much hard disk space is left. Your paging file is too small. Increasing disk space and increasing RAM will alleviate this problem.

continues

Windows Stop Codes (*continued*)

STOP CODE (0's after X truncated)	DESCRIPTION	POSSIBLE SOLUTION
0xC00135: UNABLE_TO_LOCATE_DLL	A DLL file failed to load properly.	The file may be missing or damaged. It may have been copied to a bad sector on the hard drive. Or the registry might be pointing to an invalid DLL. The error defines what file failed to load. If it is a valid DLL, extract it to the SYSTEM32 directory and try again.
0xC00218: UNKNOWN_HARD_ERROR	A registry hive file failed to load.	The registry files may be corrupted. Sometimes is caused by bad memory. Run a memory diagnostic program. If memory passes, reinstall Windows.
0xC0021A: STATUS_SYSTEM_PROCESS_TERMINATED	A user-mode sub-system has been compromised.	Either WINLOGON or CSRSS have been compromised and system security cannot be guaranteed.

Table 7.5: Common Stop Code errors

The Recovery Console

A powerful tool that is a part of Win2K and WinXP is the Recovery

For more information on Troubleshooting the Win2k Boot Process, go to page 734, Chapter 28 of *The Complete Guide to A+ Certification*.

Console. The Recovery Console contains a number of command-line utilities that are not readily available from a conventional

Windows boot. Some of the things that you can do using the Recovery Console are:

✔ Copy/rename/replace/delete/etc. operating system files and folders.
✔ Run CheckDisk against the available directories.
✔ List services and devices and their respective startup types.
✔ Enable/disable services/devices from starting during next boot sequence.
✔ Repair the boot sector or MBR.
✔ Create/format drive partitions.

There are in fact a large number of useful utilities that are only available from the Recovery Console. Among these are the following:

ATTRIB: Changes the attributes of a file or directory.

BATCH: Executes the commands specified in the text file.

BOOTCFG: Allows the user to fix the BOOT.INI file.

CHDIR (CD): Displays the name of the current directory or changes the current directory.

CHKDSK: Checks a disk and displays a status report.

CLS: Clears the screen.

COPY: Copies a single file to another location.

DELETE (DEL): Deletes one or more files.

DIR: Displays a list of files and subdirectories in a directory.

DISABLE: Disables a system service or a device driver.

DISKPART: Manages partitions on your hard drives.

ENABLE: Starts or enables a system service or a device driver.

EXIT: Exits the Recovery Console and restarts your computer.

EXPAND: Extracts a file from a compressed file.

FIXBOOT: Writes a new partition boot sector onto the system partition.

FIXMBR: Repairs the master boot record of the partition boot sector.

FORMAT: Formats a disk.

HELP: Displays a list of the commands you can use in the Recovery Console.

LISTSVC: Lists the services and drivers available on the computer.

LOGON: Logs on to a Windows 2000 installation.

MAP: Displays the drive letter mappings.

MKDIR (MD): Creates a directory.

MORE: Displays a text file.

RENAME (REN): Renames a single file.

RMDIR (RD): Deletes a directory.

SET: Displays and sets environment variables.

SYSTEMROOT: Sets the current directory to the system root directory of the system you are currently logged on to.

TYPE: Displays a text file.

For more detailed information on each of these commands, type `help [command]` (where the word command is replaced by the actual command you wish help with.) For example, `help type` will give you a description of what the command does, along with the proper syntax for using the command.

A couple of notes are in order concerning the Recovery Console. For one thing, it is a very powerful tool, and in the wrong hands a system can be rendered unbootable and sensitive data can potentially be compromised. In order to minimize the damage that can be done in this mode, Microsoft has taken a couple of protective measures.

One of these measures is to disable write access to the floppy diskette drive. The machine can read from a floppy and copy it to the hard drive, but not vice-versa. As an administrator or a service technician, you might need to be able to bypass this feature. In order to do that, click Start>Programs>Administrative Tools>Local Security Policy. Under Local Policy>Security Options, double-click Recovery Console: Allow floppy copy and access to all drives and all folders. Select Enabled, and then click OK. Reboot the machine, press F8 to get to the Advanced Boot menu and select Recovery Console. At the command prompt, type set AllowRemovableMedia = TRUE. You should now be able to write files to the floppy disk drive.

Another limitation of Recovery Console is that, in that mode, a user's access to the hard disk is restricted to the \winnt and \cmdcons directories. This can cause problems for an administrator trying to gain access to a user's files on a system he or she is trying to recover. Perform the same procedure as far as the Administrative Tools>Local Policy described above (if you haven't already done it). Once you reboot, in order to access other files at the command prompt type set AllowAllPaths = TRUE. This will open access to other directories.

The Command Prompt

The command prompt often offers tools and applications not available from the graphical interface. The following table lists a few of those and what they do. To get to the command prompt in Win98, either click Start>Programs>Accessories>MS-DOS Prompt, or more simply, click Start>Run and type command into the run line. Win2K and WinXP are basically the same, except at the run line, you would type cmd.

For more information on Working with the Command Prompt, go to page 528, Chapter 21 of *The Complete Guide to A+ Certification*.

Table 7.6 lists common command line commands

Common Command Line Commands

Command	Description	Example	Comments
ATTRIB	Displays or changes attribute to a file. + adds attribute, - removes attribute	ATTRIB FILE.DOC -R removes the Read Only attribute from FILE.DOC	R = Read Only A = Archived S = System H = Hidden

Command	Description	Example	Comments
BOOTCFG	Allows in external editing of BOOT.INI	BOOTCFG /REBUILD would take the user through a step-by-step process of creating a new BOOT.INI file	Only works on WinXP in the Recovery Console.
CACLS	Allows user to view or edit the access control list for a file	A large list of triggers to modify the command can be accessed with the /? trigger.	Only works in NT, Win2K, and WinXP.
CD or CHDIR	Change Directory	CD\WINDOWS goes to the Windows directory.	A backslash after the command takes you to a subdirectory of the root; no backslash takes you to a subdirectory of the current directory.
CHKDSK	Checks drive for errors	CHKDSK A: checks drive A for errors.	Can fix crosslinked files and certain FAT errors.
CLS	Clears the screen	CLS	Returns a blank screen with only a single command prompt line.
COPY	Copy files from source location to target location; uses wildcards	COPY A:\FILE.DOC C:\My Documents	Transfers an exact copy of the data in the source file to the target location.
D:	Go to drive D	F: takes you to the F drive	If you've already visited the target drive and left off in a directory, on subsequent visits you will return to the same directory.
DEL	Deletes files	DEL FILE.DOC	Removes FILE.DOC from current directory.
DELTREE	Deletes an entire directory and all subdirectories within	DELTREE C:\FILES removes the FILES directory and all files and subdirectories within.	Is *not* recoverable by standard utilities!
DIR	Lists files in directory; asterisk acts as wildcard	DIR	List all files in current directory.
		DIR *.HTM	List all files with HTM extension.
		DIR /S	List all files in current directory and all directories below current directory.
		DIR /W	Shows file names only, five columns across screen.
		DIR /P	Fills screen and then pauses until user presses a key.
FC	File comparison utility	FC NOVEL.DOC WEIRD.DOC compares those two files and displays the differences.	A number of different triggers defining what to look for can be accessed with the /? trigger.
FDISK	Prepares a new disk to accept data	FDISK	This is not a reversible process. Cannot be performed on the same drive from which it is run.

continues

Common Command-Line Commands (*continued*)

Command	Description	Example	Comments
FIND	Finds text in a file	FIND "Billy Bob" FILE.TXT	Displays each line in FILE.TXT that contains the text in quotes.
FIXBOOT	Restores boot sector to Win2K and WinXP drives	FIXBOOT C: restores boot sector to drive C:	Works only from the recovery console in Win2K and WinXP.
FORMAT	Formats a drive	FORMAT A: formats the A: drive.	/q trigger does a quick format.
FIXMBR	Restores master boot record to Win2K and WinXP drives	FIXBOOT C: restores master boot record to drive C:	Works only from the recovery console in Win2K and WinXP.
IPCONFIG	Shows the TCP/IP configuration for the computer	IPCONFIG /ALL shows the total configuration. IPCONFIG /RELEASE erases the TCP/IP configuration in computers configured to use DHCP. IPCONFIG /RENEW adds a new TCP/IP configuration to computers configured to use DHCP.	Only available on computers with TCP/IP installed.
NETSTAT	Shows a list of all network connections to computer	NETSTAT -e shows all Ethernet connections	Only works on computers with TCP/IP installed. A large number of triggers is displayed with the /? trigger.
NSLOOKUP	Looks up IP address of a domain or host on a network	NSLOOKUP GRAVES2 locates and displays the IP address of a computer named GRAVES2.	Only works on computers with TCP/IP installed. A large number of triggers is displayed with the /? trigger.
RD	Removes a directory	RD TEMP removes the TEMP directory.	Backslash after command directs it to root directory; no backslash works in current directory.
REN	Renames files	REN FILE.DOC FILE.BAK	Renames FILE.DOC to FILE.BAK.
ROUTE	Shows routing tables	ROUTE PRINT sends routing table to screen.	Only works on computers with TCP/IP installed. A large number of triggers is displayed with the /? trigger.
SORT	Sorts the lines within a text file	SORT EMAIL.TXT	Sorts each line in the file EMAIL.TXT.
XCOPY	Like copy, but works with entire directories	XCOPY C:\FILES A:\ moves all files and subdirectories of the C:\FILES folder to drive A:	Has a large number of triggers to customize command. Type XCOPY /? for listing.

Table 7.6: Common commands and their triggers

Part 8

Networking Issues

While this is not targeted primarily to be a book on networking, we live in a day when all computer professionals need to have some familiarity with the subject. This section covers some of the basic knowledge you'll need to get by in networking.

Making Your Own Patch Cables

One tool no serious computer technician should be without is a decent crimping tool for making network cables. For certain, it's far too easy and cheap these days to buy ready-made cables over at the electronics store. Still, there comes a time when the store isn't available, despite how badly you need a cable. Having a roll of CAT5e cable and a bag of RJ-45 connectors in your toolbox can make you a hero.

If you open a standard twisted-pair cable, you'll see four pairs of wires, and each of these pairs is twisted together. Bet you know why they call it twisted pair now, don't you? The colors you see on each strand of wire is not random. The Electronics Industry Association, in conjunction with the Telecommunications Industry Association, developed a standard color code for cables. These colors are:

> For more information on Bounded Media, go to page 805, Chapter 32 of *The Complete Guide to A+ Certification.*

✔ Pair 1 = Orange - White/Orange striped
✔ Pair 2 = Green - White/Green striped
✔ Pair 3 = Blue - White/Blue striped
✔ Pair 4 = Brown - White/Brown striped

Unfortunately, they couldn't agree on a single set of standards for wiring patch cables. There are in fact two standard wiring configurations used. Fortunately, the only way they differ lies in which pairs of cable carry the voltage. For the most part, the vast majority of manufacturers follow the 568B standards for most products they carry. However, as you might imagine, you will run into difficulties if you guess wrong. **Table 8.1** lists the two standards.

EIA/TIA 568A and 568B standards for twisted-pair cabling

Pin No.	Signal Carried	568B	568A
1	Transmit (+)	White/Orange	White/Green
2	Transmit (-)	Orange	Green
3	Receive (+)	White/Green	White/Orange
4	Not Used	Blue	Blue
5	Not Used	White/Blue	White/Blue
6	Receive (-)	Green	Orange
7	Not Used	White/Brown	White/Brown
8	Not Used	Brown	Brown

Table 8.1: As you'll notice, the only way the two standards differ is in the colors used for voltage carrying wires.

A standard cable is used whenever a device is being hooked up to a hub or a switch. It would not work in directly connecting two devices. Hooking two devices would include interconnecting two NICs directly, without benefit of a hub or switch, or when connecting a laptop or other device to the configuration port on a router. To do this, you need a crossover cable. To wire a crossover cable, use the wiring diagram in **Table 8.2.**

Wiring Diagram for Crossover Cable

Pin No. End 1	Signal Transmitted (device)	569A Color Coding	568B Color Coding	Pin No. End 2	Signal Received (device)
1	Transmit (+)	White/Green	White/Orange	3	Receive (+)
2	Transmit (-)	Green	Orange	6	Receive (-)
3	Receive (+)	White/Orange	White/Green	1	Transmit (+)
4	Not Used	Blue	Blue	4	Not Used
5	Not Used	White/Blue	White/Blue	5	Not Used
6	Receive (-)	Orange	Green	2	Transmit (-)
7	Not Used	White/Brown	White/Brown	7	Not Used
8	Not Used	Brown	Brown	8	Not Used

Table 8.2: If you need to directly interconnect two devices, you'll need a crossover cable. This wiring pinout shows you how to make your own.

Troubleshooting Network Issues

In Part 1 of this book, I listed a formal troubleshooting approach. I would like to add one "unofficial" step that makes particular sense

> For more information on Operating Systems and Networking, go to page 833, Chapter 33 of *The Complete Guide to A+ Certification.*

in network issues. Before you start stretching your brain for technical solutions, look for the obvious first. A very large percentage of problems

that you see on a day-to-day basis are common problems. And common problems have obvious solutions. Some of the obvious items to check include the following:

✔ Eliminate user error. Issues like Caps Lock and Num Lock keys can prevent the user from logging on.

✔ Check for power.

✔ Check the cables. Is the power cable is plugged into the wall? Now go a step further. Is it plugged into the computer? Is the surge suppressor looped back and plugged into itself? Check the network cable as well. For some reason, users find it difficult to log on when the patch cable is dangling in the air.

✔ Check for blinky lights. Link lights on hubs and NICs indicate that you have electrical connectivity. The color of lights on devices can have varying meanings. Green is good; amber is usually not so good.

✔ Check for logical connectivity. Ping the Server. If that fails, ping the router interface (if one exists). Then ping the NIC itself. If you have a statically configured IP address, pinging that IP address confirms that TCP/IP is working. Pinging 127.0.0.1 tells you the NIC is working.

Most operating systems these days come with a fairly elaborate collection of software tools built in. Before you start talking about spending large

> For more information on Configuring TCP/IP, go to page 850, Chapter 33 of *The Complete Guide to A+ Certification.*

amounts of money on some third-party utility, you should probably consider whether one of these built-in tools might do the job.

Most networks use the TCP/IP protocol, and there are a number of useful diagnostic utilities built into the protocol. Whether you're running Windows or Linux, these are at your disposal.

TCP/IP Utilities

Windows Command	Linux Command	Purpose
ping	ping	Confirms a connection between two devices.
tracert	traceroute	Lists all interfaces between here and there.

continues

TCP/IP Utilities (*continued*)

Windows Command	Linux Command	Purpose
netstat	netstat	Reports all outside connections to a specific interface.
route	route	Lists or modifies the routing tables of a local machine.
nbtstat	nbtstat	Lists current IP connections to an interface as well as other protocol statistics.
ipconfig	ifconfig	Displays the configuration for the interfaces on a device.

Table 8.3: The TCP/IP protocol comes complete with its own set of diagnostics utilities.

For more information on TCP/IP Utilities, go to page 852, Chapter 33 of *The Complete Guide to A+ Certification.*

For a little more detail on each of these utilities, read on.

PING

Syntax: `ping -trigger -trigger 127.0.0.1`

or

`ping -trigger -trigger www.mywebsite.com`

The PING Command

Trigger	Description	Notes
-a	Resolves IP address to host name	Tells you the target computer's NetBIOS name if connection is made.
-t	Keeps pinging target device until stopped	<Ctrl>+<Break> displays statistics and continues, <Ctrl>+C stops continuous ping.
-n number	Specifies number of echo requests to send	Number is replaced by how many times you want to ping the target.
-l size	Sets the send buffer size	Size is replaced by the desired size of the buffer file in bytes.
-f	Don't send a fragment flag in the packet	Routers along the Internet may not break this packet up for any reason.
-l ttl	Set time to live for packets	Replace ttl with desired time in milliseconds.

Trigger	Description	Notes
-v tos	Sets the Type of Service	Must be a value between 0 and 255. See RFC 1349 for a listing of these values.
-r count	Records the number of hops	Similar to tracert command.
-w timeout	Specifies timeout before dropping packet	Timeout is replaced by desired value in milliseconds.

Table 8.4: Triggers for the PING command

TRACERT

Syntax: `tracert -trigger -trigger 127.0.0.1`

or

`tracert -trigger -trigger www.mywebsite.com`

The TRACERT Command

Trigger	Description	Notes
-d	Do not resolve addresses to host names	Default is to resolve.
-h	Limits the number of hops to search for a target address	By default, the command will search for up to 32 hops.
-j	Provides a loose source route and host list	The host list displays each host's computer name and IP address.
-w timeout	Specifies a specific timeout before dropping packet	Where timeout is specified in milliseconds.

Table 8.5: Triggers for the TRACERT command

NETSTAT

Syntax: `netstat -trigger -trigger`

The NETSTAT Command

Trigger	Description	Notes
-a	Displays all open connections and ports	Lists the active protocols and connections by NetBIOS name.
-e	Lists only Ethernet connection statistics	Can be used in conjunction with –s (below).
-n	Displays addresses and connections in numerical form	Lists IP addresses and ports in hexadecimal. Easier to read.
-p protocol	Displays statistics only for specified protocol	The word protocol in the example is replaced with a specific protocol, such as `netstat -p udp`.
-r	Displays routing table	Only display static routing tables.
Interval	Scans all interfaces and redisplays new statistics as specified intervals	Interval is specified in seconds. <Ctrl>+C stops scanning.

Table 8.6: Triggers for the NETSTAT command

ROUTE

Syntax: `route -trigger -trigger`

The ROUTE Command

Trigger	Description	Notes
-f	Clears routing tables	If used in conjunction with another command, the clearing occurs prior to executing the other command.
-p	Makes route persistent	If the machine is restarted, these routes will be retained after reboot.
PRINT	Displays routing tables on screen	Can be used in conjunction with other triggers.
DELETE	Deletes all routing tables	Can be used with the * as a wildcard to delete specific entries.
NETMASK	Specifies a subnet mask for the current entry	Non-IP address values will result in error.

Table 8.7: Triggers for the ROUTE command

NBTSTAT

Syntax: `nbtstat -trigger -trigger`

The NBTSTAT Command

Trigger	Description	Notes
-a computer-name	NetBIOS Adapter status	Lists the remote machine's name table when given its name.
-A ipaddress	NetBIOS Adapter status	Lists the remote machine's name table when given its IP address.
-c	Lists the NBT cache of the remote host	Lists names and IP addresses.
-n	Lists local NetBIOS names	All connections to local LAN connection are listed.
-r	Lists NetBIOS names resolved by broadcast or WINS	WINS connections are listed by Name Server.
-R	Reload	Purges and reloads the name table cache.
-S	Session Tables	Lists all open sessions by IP address.
-s	Session Tables	Lists all open sessions, converting IP address to NetBIOS name.
RR	Refresh and Release	Sends Release packets to the WINS server then refreshes tables.

Table 8.8: Triggers for the NBTSTAT command

IPCONFIG

Syntax: `ipconfig -trigger -trigger`

The IPCONFIG Command

Trigger	Description	Notes
-all	Detailed configuration listing	Shows complete IP configuration for all interfaces on machine.
-release	Releases DHCP configured addresses	Not available on statically configured interfaces.
-renew	Registers a new DHCP configuration	Not available on statically configured interfaces.
-flushdns	Empties the DNS resolver cache	Can slow down the performance in network browsing until cache is rebuilt.

continues

The IPCONFIG Command (*continued*)

Trigger	Description	Notes
-registerdns	Rebuilds DHCP settings	Refreshes all DHCP leases and renews DNS name registration.
-displaydns	Displays the contents of the DNS resolver cache	Would be a more useful utility if it offered a pause function.

Table 8.9: Triggers for the IPCONFIG command

Logon Issues

When a user fails to log on successfully, there are a variety of reasons that may have caused the situation. The most common one is that even the best of us occasionally fat-finger our password and it gets rejected by the server. Servers can be configured to lock an account out after so many failed attempts. They can also be set to allow a limited number of simultaneous logons. If the user cannot log on to a client/server-based network, check for the following issues:

✔ **Is the Caps Lock key on?** Passwords are case-sensitive, and even if you type the password using the correct set of numbers and letters, if you're using uppercase in place of lowercase (or vice versa) the password will be rejected.

✔ **Is the Num Lock key on?** If there are numbers in your password, and you are using the keypad to type those numbers, the light should be glowing. If not, you're not really typing the numbers. You only think you are.

✔ **Is the user logged on to multiple workstations?** Networks can be configured to allow a limited number of simultaneous logons. Once the user reaches that limit, it doesn't matter how accurately he or she types the password. The server won't authenticate that user again.

✔ **Did multiple failed logons lock out the account?** This one is easy to figure out once you type in a valid user ID/password combination. The system will *tell* you you're locked out.

✔ **On a Novell network, are you logging on to the correct tree?** Larger networks may have multiple trees, and you might be assigned to a specific one.

Part 9

Diagnosing Printer Problems

Printers come in a wide variety of makes and models, but they can basically be broken down into three types. Impact printers consist of dot matrix and line printers. Inkjets come in both solid and liquid ink varieties. Optical printers use either LEDs or (more commonly) laser diodes to do their work.

When a printer isn't working right, it can be every bit as frustrating as when a computer malfunctions. Especially when your *Pocket Guide* manuscript is due at the publisher in just a few days! There are a few problems related to all printers, regardless of type. Then there are those that are specific to a particular type of printer. This is a generic guide and does not pretend to cover all the problems you'll find. The service manual to my old LaserJet 4 is 240 pages long. I have to keep this shorter than that.

General Printer Problems

Just like when anything on a computer, or anywhere else for that matter, stops working, start by checking the basics.

Start with the Basics

As with any other device I've discussed in this book, always check the cables first. You'd be amazed how often wires just pop off the back of a machine. And printers do get moved around a lot. They get shuffled every time you add paper, every time you change toner or ink cartridges, and, for those of you neat freaks who actually dust once in a while,

For more information on Printing Technologies, go to page 435, Chapter 18 of *The Complete Guide to A+ Certification.* when you're on a cleaning binge. A loose power cable will prevent the printer from powering on, while a loose data cable blocks print jobs.

Next check the printer queue. In Windows, you do that by clicking Start→Settings→Printers and then double-clicking the icon for the printer in question. If a job is locked up, it prevents other jobs from passing through, and, as far as users are concerned, the printer isn't working. If you see a job hung in the queue, highlight the offending job, click the Document menu, and then click Cancel. If the job doesn't want to go away, click Printer→Cancel All Documents. It can take several minutes for the jobs to be cleared, so be patient.

With many models of inkjet printers and a few laser printers, some-times a printer just sits there like a bump on a log after you send a job to it. It doesn't print, but it doesn't respond with any error messages either. This is frequently accompanied by one or more flashing LEDs. Quite often this can be fixed with a simple reboot. Unplug the printer from the wall, count to thirty (slowly), and then plug the printer back in. This forces a hard reset of the printer that simply turning it off and back on won't accomplish.

If you are unable to print, or an error message reports, "There is an error writing to LPT1" (or other port), there are a couple of things to look for. If you just installed the printer, make sure you have the proper cable. Most new printers require an IEEE-1284 cable. If you've just added a new printer to an old system and the printer isn't recognized, verify that you are using the correct cable.

For more information on IEEE 1284, go to page 453, Chapter 18 of *The Complete Guide to A+ Certification*.

On a system that connects via a USB port, and that doesn't have any other USB devices, check the CMOS settings to make sure that USB is enabled. If the CMOS shows USB up and running, go to Control Panel→Device Manager and verify that the USB drivers are loaded and operational.

Is It the Printer or Is It the Computer?

When a printer quits working, one of the first questions you have to ask is "Is it the printer, or is it the computer(s) the printer is hooked up to?"

First of all, see if the printer is working correctly by itself. You can remove the computer from the process temporarily by doing the following:

1. Make sure the printer is turned on, that there is paper in the paper tray, and that there is no paper jammed in the printer.
2. Disconnect the printer cable from the printer.

3. Print a self-test page. Depending on your model, this may be done using one of the following methods:
   - Hold down the resume (On-Line) button for three or four seconds.
   - Press the menu button until you locate Print Test Page.
   - Hold down the resume button while powering on the printer.

It should print out a sample test page.

If the printer prints out a test page, then you've ruled out the printer as the problem. Next thing you will want to test is the cable. Check the cable length. Ideally, a printer cable should be no longer than ten feet. Fifteen-foot cables are generally acceptable in areas that are relatively free of electromagnetic interference. Anything longer than that should be avoided. If possible, try swapping out the cable with a known-good cable. Reattach the cable and make sure it is firmly connected to the printer and the computer.

If your printer is hooked up to the parallel port, you can also try printing from a command prompt. This bypasses Windows drivers for the time being.

1. Click Start.
2. Select Shut Down (or Turn Off Computer).
3. Select Restart.
4. While the system is restarting, press the F8 key repeatedly every couple of seconds. This will bring up a startup menu.
5. Select Command prompt only from the list. When the computer finishes booting, you'll be at a C: prompt.
6. From the command prompt, type `dir > lpt1` and press <Enter>. This command will send a directory list to your printer.

If the list prints, then you know that the port is working. If it does not, you may need to check your BIOS settings to make sure the port is set up correctly. Check the section in this book on BIOS configuration. To restart your computer in Normal mode, press the reset button on your computer, or power off the computer and power it back on again.

If the latter test was successful, there may be a driver conflict in Windows that is preventing the printer from working. Remove the printer driver and re-install it. Make sure you have the driver disks that shipped with your printer. If you don't have the disks, you will probably be able to download the files from the manufacturer's Web site.

Ugly Character Syndrome

Another problem common to all printer types is the mysterious ugly character syndrome. The printer prints. It just doesn't print what you want it to. Either the entire print job looks like this: $\prod \pm$ ó @, or a few weird characters appear at the top or along the sides of the page. A variation of this theme is a single line at the top of about six hundred pages, when all you printed was a single page of text.

This is almost always the result of an incorrect or a corrupted printer driver. Delete the printer from the Printer applet in Control Panel or from System Preferences on your Mac, and re-install a new set of drivers. Make sure you're using the correct ones.

Dot Matrix Printer Issues

Since dot matrix printers are almost purely mechanical devices, they require significantly more care and feeding than most other components in a system. Unfortunately, they're all too often the devices that get the least attention. As a result, many dot matrix printers don't enjoy nearly as long a lifespan as they should be able to expect. That they last as long as they do is a tribute to the manufacturers!

For more information on Impact Printers, go to page 436, Chapter 18 of *The Complete Guide to A+ Certification*.

Keep It Clean

The condition of both the platen and the print heads directly impacts print quality. If too much dried ink and paper fiber gets jammed into the print head, the pins might not be ejected by the springs. This results in sketchy print quality. A dirty or damaged platen can be just as harmful. Never let somebody send a print job onto a dot matrix printer when there's no paper installed. Pay attention to the warnings the printer issues saying it's out of paper. On dot matrix printers, if you send a print job despite the warning, the print head will stream along, sending the print job to the platen, polluting it with ink and perhaps even punching holes into the hard rubber. If there are holes in the platen, the pins will punch through the paper, putting holes in your page. If there is ink on the platen, the back of your page will be covered with stray marks.

Keep It Aligned

Improper alignment of the print head: If the print head is not properly aligned, individual characters will shade from light to dark. **Figure 9.1** illustrates what can happen if the print head itself is out of alignment.

The figure shows a vertical alignment problem, but print heads can be offset either vertically or horizontally.

A print
head out
of line.

Figure 9.1   A print head out of alignment affects individual letters.

An improperly aligned platen: If the platen itself goes out of alignment the entire line will be affected. It will go from light at the beginning of the line to dark at the end, or vice versa. **Figure 9.2** shows what I mean.

A Platen
out of line.

Figure 9.2   A platen out of alignment throws the whole line out of whack!

As far as realigning either the head or the platen, how that is done or even whether or not it can be done depends on the make and model of your printer. Most print heads can be aligned. With many models, aligning the platen is a factory service job. If you can get your hands on a service manual for your model, it should give you instructions on how to perform these tasks.

Inkjet Printer Issues

Inkjet printers have become so cheap these days you can almost consider them to be a disposable commodity. Why spend a hundred bucks

For more information on Inkjet Technologies, go to page 440, Chapter 18 of *The Complete Guide to A+ Certification*.

fixing a printer when it only costs you eighty bucks to buy a new one at the store? Even so, there are a few things you can do to keep your printer going a day or two longer, and to make sure print quality is as good as it can be.

General Inkjet Issues

General beeping after installing a new cartridge: The cartridge isn't installed correctly. Make sure all cartridges snap into their wells firmly. Still no go? You know that piece of tape covering the print heads? You were supposed to take that off. You did, didn't you?

No output whatsoever: You did remember the ink cartridges, right? The printer doesn't ship with those installed. If the printer has been unused for quite some time, it's also possible that the ink has dried up in the print head nozzles. Try running the print head cleaning utility that shipped with the printer. If the printer has been sitting for a very long time, you might have to give it a boost. Remove the ink cartridges and *very gently* swab down the print head around the nozzles with a cotton swab dabbed in alcohol. If that fails, you might need to replace the ink cartridges altogether.

You turn the printer on and it goes into a state of perpetual initialization: Either the ink cartridges are not properly installed or the tape is still on the print heads.

Print Quality Issues in Inkjets

Generally fuzzy output: Can be the result of print heads out of alignment. This most frequently occurs with newly installed ink cartridges. Run the alignment utility that ships with the printer.

White streaks across the output: Some of the nozzles in the print head are clogged. Run the cleaning utility and/or use the cotton swab/alcohol treatment.

Colors are printing in a distinct off-color: One or more of the color inks has run out. Replace the ink cartridge (or the appropriate color). Your printer management utility can tell you which cartridge to replace if there are multiple cartridges. Also check the dithering options in your printer driver. Some printers don't print well with dithering enabled. Try turning it off.

Images exhibit serious banding: Horizontal striping, or banding, as it is called, can be the result of several things. If it happens on some types of paper and not others, the paper showing the problem is not suitable for your printer. If it happens across the board, clean the print heads. Another thing that causes banding is having the wrong printer settings configured in the driver. Check your manual for the proper settings for the type of work you're doing and the media you're using.

Paper Feed or Carriage Problems

The carriage does not return to a full left position: Most often, this is a result of the ink cartridges not being properly installed. Make sure all cartridges are fully seated in their wells. If this is not the problem, check the paper feed switch. This is a small lever with virtually no resistance positioned near the paper input. If it doesn't move freely, it needs to be replaced.

Carriage stops in the middle of a print job, then ejects paper: Same problem as above.

Paper jams: When paper gets jammed in an inkjet, be very careful not to just yank it out. Leaving shreds of paper behind can permanently damage the printer.

✔ Make sure that you are using the correct paper. Photo paper that is not designed for an inkjet will not only smear badly, it can jam easily.

✔ If you are using glossy paper, make sure that the glossy side faces the correct direction. Feed rollers can have a hard time gripping a glossy surface.

✔ Be careful not to use paper that is too heavy for your printer. The specifications tell you how heavy a paper you can use.

Multiple pages feed at once: The most common cause for this problem is either incorrect media, or media that has been subjected to improper storage. Inkjets rely on a friction feed mechanism. If paper is too dry or too moist, it sticks together. Also, do not overfill the input tray. This causes multiple feeds.

> *A Note on Recycling Ink and Toner Cartridges:* A thriving business has developed around the ecologically sound principle of recycling ink and toner cartridges. There is also a bit of controversy over the idea. Since you are unlikely to get an unbiased discussion from either the printer manufacturers (who want to sell you their new cartridges) or the recyclers (who want you to buy their product), I thought I'd throw in my two cents. The cost savings of refilling your own ink cartridges or purchasing remanufactured toner cartridges are substantial. However, along with those savings come some inherent tradeoffs.

With ink cartridges, drying time, mixing characteristics, and the weight of the ink mix are important factors in color and print quality. Another thing to consider is the logic chip embedded in the cartridge. If the remanufacturer doesn't replace the chip with every refill, you might end up with a situation where the inks don't get properly distributed the way the printer driver tells them to. As a result, the print quality delivered by remanufactured ink cartridges can range from fairly decent (but not as good as the original) to abysmal.

Manufacturers claim that the use of these remanufactured cartridges shortens the life of the printer. While I have located no detailed research to confirm this claim, I can see how this is theoretically possible. The inkjet process centers on the ink, and since the ink used in the remanufacturing process is thinner, this would have an impact on the rest of the printing mechanism. The seals must be punctured in order to insert the inks into the cartridge, and if the seals are not properly restored, the cartridge can burst, spewing ink into the printer. This is rare, but I have seen the results of this happening, and it isn't pretty. Colorful, but not pretty.

There are fewer risks involved in the use of remanufactured toner cartridges, and with one notable exception, these risks all center on print quality and not the life of the printer. In order to produce the fine resolution that modern laser printers are capable of, the particles used in the manufacture of the toner must be correspondingly smaller. Many remanufacturers take the "one size fits all" approach to toner refills, which will show up in the reproduction of graphics. Other issues affecting print quality involve the proper replacement of different components in the cartridge. A damaged imaging drum or a faulty cleaning blade that doesn't get replaced will cause print defects. The notable exception that can affect the life of the printer is in how well the remanufacturer refits the seals. As with the inkjet cartridges, if a seal in a toner cartridge bursts, the effects can be disastrous.

However, the risks involved are low-percentage risks. Disaster is extremely rare, so it's like the reverse of playing the lottery. If lower print quality is not an issue, recycling toner and ink cartridges can save money and is friendly on the environment. But before you make the jump to recycled products on a newer printer, check and see if there is any fine print in the warranty concerning their use.

Laser Printer Issues

General printer issues are the same for laser printers as they are other printer types. In terms of print quality and paper feed issues, they have a few issues unique to the their kind. To fully understand some of the parts I'll be discussing in the next section, I strongly recommend you read the "Components of the Laser Printer" section in Chapter 18, Printing Technologies, in *The Complete Guide to A+ Certification*.

For more information on Optical Printers, go to page 444, Chapter 18 of *The Complete Guide to A+ Certification*.

Print Defects in Laser Printers

Repetitive defects: Stray marks that occur at regular intervals down the page are caused by one of the rollers in the printer. Manufacturers provide a repetitive defect ruler with their service manuals that help you identify exactly which roller is the culprit. Since most people won't be walking around with a service manual for their printer in their pockets, here is a general guide. The transfer roller usually causes defects that are fairly close together. Defects that appear twice on the page are usually the result of an unruly fusing assembly. Single defects that appear on all pages can be blamed on the imaging drum, which on most printers is part of the toner cartridge.

Smeared output: This problem can be rough to diagnose. The most prominent cause is that the cleaning blade is not removing all residual toner from the imaging drum. You see this a lot on recycled toner cartridges. Replace the toner cartridge. A faulty transfer roller can also cause smears. Never touch the transfer roller. If you attempt to clean it, do so with the cleaning brush that shipped with the printer. Steel wool is **not** the answer here. You will also see this symptom when the fuser assembly is on its way out.

Toner is flaking off: This is caused by a fuser assembly that no longer heats to full temperature. Replace the fuser.

Spilled toner: Check for broken seals. Using an antistatic vacuum, clean up all spilled toner. If you have no other choice, swab as much of it up with a *lightly* dampened cloth as you can. Let it dry and blow out the rest with compressed air. Replace the offending toner cartridge.

Paper comes out blank: Did you just replace the toner? Don't you hate it when you forget to remove the tape that seals the toner cartridge in shipping? Remove the tape and try again. If the toner cartridge is properly installed, either your controller board has failed or you don't have sufficient voltage going to your transfer roller. Either way, the printer requires professional service.

Paper prints all black: If you're lucky, all that's happening is that the primary charging roller is defective. That's not as bad as it sounds, since that roller is part of the toner cartridge. If replacing the toner cartridge doesn't fix the problem, then it is likely the controller board. That requires professional service.

Paper Feed Problems in Laser Printers

Paper jams: Laser printers have a number of different rollers that are user-replaceable. Check the rollers in the general area of the jam for excessive wear. Paper jams in the output area can be caused by a worn or defective diverter assembly. This would require professional service.

Multiple pages are picked up: Laser printers have either a separator pad or a separator roller to pick up the top page and leave the next one behind. Check for wear and replace if necessary. Pickup rollers can also be the culprits.

Creased pages: Most generally, this is caused by improper media or media that has been improperly stored. Also, if you print labels from time to time, it is possible for a label to come loose from the page and get left behind.

Index

W

Notes